Travel phrasebooks collection
«Everything Will Be Okay!»

T&P Books Publishing

PHRASEBOOK
INDONESIAN

I0163383

THE MOST IMPORTANT PHRASES

This phrasebook contains
the most important
phrases and questions
for basic communication
Everything you need
to survive overseas

By Andrey Taranov

T&P BOOKS

Phrasebook + 1500-word dictionary

English-Indonesian phrasebook & concise dictionary

By Andrey Taranov

The collection of "Everything Will Be Okay" travel phrasebooks published by T&P Books is designed for people traveling abroad for tourism and business. The phrasebooks contain what matters most - the essentials for basic communication. This is an indispensable set of phrases to "survive" while abroad.

Another section of the book also provides a small dictionary with more than 1,500 useful words arranged alphabetically. The dictionary includes a lot of gastronomic terms and will be helpful when ordering food at a restaurant or buying groceries at the store.

T&P Books Publishing
www.tpbooks.com

ISBN: 978-1-78616-748-4

This book is also available in E-book formats.
Please visit www.tpbooks.com or the major online bookstores.

FOREWORD

The collection of "Everything Will Be Okay" travel phrasebooks published by T&P Books is designed for people traveling abroad for tourism and business. The phrasebooks contain what matters most - the essentials for basic communication. This is an indispensable set of phrases to "survive" while abroad.

This phrasebook will help you in most cases where you need to ask something, get directions, find out how much something costs, etc. It can also resolve difficult communication situations where gestures just won't help.

This book contains a lot of phrases that have been grouped according to the most relevant topics. A separate section of the book also provides a small dictionary with more than 1,500 important and useful words.

Take "Everything Will Be Okay" phrasebook with you on the road and you'll have an irreplaceable traveling companion who will help you find your way out of any situation and teach you to not fear speaking with foreigners.

TABLE OF CONTENTS

T&P Books Publishing

PRONUNCIATION

Letter	Indonesian example	T&P phonetic alphabet	English example
Aa	zaman	[a]	shorter than in ask
Bb	besar	[b]	baby, book
Cc	kecil, cepat	[ʧ]	church, French
Dd	dugaan	[d]	day, doctor
Ee	segera, mencium	[e], [ə]	medal, elm
Ff	berfungsi	[f]	face, food
Gg	juga, lagi	[g]	game, gold
Hh	hanya, bahwa	[h]	home, have
Ii	izin, sebagai ganti	[i], [j]	Peter, yard
Jj	setuju, ijin	[dʒ]	jeans, gin
Kk	kemudian, tidak	[k], [']	kiss, glottal stop
Ll	dilarang	[l]	lace, people
Mm	melihat	[m]	magic, milk
Nn	berenang	[n], [ŋ]	name, ring
Oo	toko roti	[o:]	fall, bomb
Pp	peribahasa	[p]	pencil, private
Qq	Aquarius	[k]	clock, kiss
Rr	ratu, riang	[r]	trilled [r]
Ss	sendok, syarat	[s], [ʃ]	city, machine
Tt	tamu, adat	[t]	tourist, trip
Uu	ambulans	[u]	book
Vv	renovasi	[v]	very, river
Ww	pariwisata	[w]	vase, winter
Xx	boxer	[ks]	box, taxi
Yy	banyak, syarat	[j]	yes, New York
Zz	zamrud	[z]	zebra, please

Combinations of letters

aa	maaf	[aʾa]	a+glottal stop
kh	khawatir	[h]	home, have
th	Gereja Lutheran	[t]	tourist, trip
-k	tidak	[']	glottal stop

LIST OF ABBREVIATIONS

English abbreviations

ab.	-	about
adj	-	adjective
adv	-	adverb
anim.	-	animate
as adj	-	attributive noun used as adjective
e.g.	-	for example
etc.	-	et cetera
fam.	-	familiar
fem.	-	feminine
form.	-	formal
inanim.	-	inanimate
masc.	-	masculine
math	-	mathematics
mil.	-	military
n	-	noun
pl	-	plural
pron.	-	pronoun
sb	-	somebody
sing.	-	singular
sth	-	something
v aux	-	auxiliary verb
vi	-	intransitive verb
vi, vt	-	intransitive, transitive verb
vt	-	transitive verb

INDONESIAN PHRASEBOOK

This section contains important phrases that may come in handy in various real-life situations.
The phrasebook will help you ask for directions, clarify a price, buy tickets, and order food at a restaurant

T&P Books Publishing

PHRASEBOOK CONTENTS

T&P Books Publishing

Excuse me, …	**Permisi, …** [permisi, …]
Hello.	**Halo.** [halo]
Thank you.	**Terima kasih.** [terima kasih]
Good bye.	**Selamat tinggal.** [slamat tiŋgal]
Yes.	**Ya.** [ja]
No.	**Tidak.** [tidaʔ]
I don't know.	**Saya tidak tahu.** [saja tidaʔ tahu]
Where? | Where to? | When?	**Di mana? | Ke mana? | Kapan?** [di mana? | ke mana? | kapan?]

I need …	**Saya perlu …** [saja perlu …]
I want …	**Saya ingin …** [saja iŋin …]
Do you have …?	**Apa Anda punya …?** [apa anda punja …?]
Is there a … here?	**Apa ada … di sini?** [apa ada … di sini?]
May I …?	**Boleh saya …?** [boleh saja …?]
…, please (polite request)	**Tolong, …** [toloŋ, …]

I'm looking for …	**Saya sedang mencari …** [saja sedaŋ mentʃari …]
restroom	**kamar kecil** [kamar ketʃil]
ATM	**ATM** [a-te-em]
pharmacy (drugstore)	**apotek** [apoteʔ]
hospital	**rumah sakit** [rumah sakit]
police station	**kantor polisi** [kantor polisi]
subway	**stasiun bawah tanah** [stasiun bawah tanah]

taxi	**taksi** [taksi]
train station	**stasiun kereta api** [stasiun kereta api]

My name is …	**Nama saya …** [nama saja …]
What's your name?	**Siapa nama Anda?** [siapa nama anda?]
Could you please help me?	**Bisakah Anda menolong saya?** [bisakah anda menoloŋ saja?]
I've got a problem.	**Saya sedang kesulitan.** [saja sedaŋ kesulitan]
I don't feel well.	**Saya tidak enak badan.** [saja tida' enak badan]
Call an ambulance!	**Panggil ambulans!** [paŋgil ambulans!]
May I make a call?	**Boleh saya menelepon?** [boleh saja menelepon?]

I'm sorry.	**Maaf.** [ma'af]
You're welcome.	**Terima kasih kembali.** [terima kasih kembali]

I, me	**Saya, aku** [saja, aku]
you (inform.)	**kamu, kau** [kamu, kau]
he	**dia, ia** [dia, ia]
she	**dia, ia** [dia, ia]
they (masc.)	**mereka** [mereka]
they (fem.)	**mereka** [mereka]
we	**kami** [kami]
you (pl)	**kalian** [kalian]
you (sg, form.)	**Anda** [anda]

ENTRANCE	**MASUK** [masu']
EXIT	**KELUAR** [keluar]
OUT OF ORDER	**TIDAK DAPAT DIGUNAKAN** [tida' dapat digunakan]
CLOSED	**TUTUP** [tutup]

OPEN

BUKA
[buka]

FOR WOMEN

UNTUK PEREMPUAN
[untu' perempuan]

FOR MEN

UNTUK LAKI-LAKI
[untu' laki-laki]

Questions

Where?	**Di mana?** [di mana?]
Where to?	**Ke mana?** [ke mana?]
Where from?	**Dari mana?** [dari mana?]
Why?	**Kenapa?** [kenapa?]
For what reason?	**Untuk apa?** [untu' apa?]
When?	**Kapan?** [kapan?]
How long?	**Berapa lama?** [berapa lama?]
At what time?	**Jam berapa?** [dʒjam berapa?]
How much?	**Berapa harganya?** [berapa harganja?]
Do you have ...?	**Apa Anda punya ...?** [apa anda punja ...?]
Where is ...?	**Di mana ...?** [di mana ...?]
What time is it?	**Jam berapa sekarang?** [dʒjam berapa sekaraŋ?]
May I make a call?	**Boleh saya menelepon?** [boleh saja menelepon?]
Who's there?	**Siapa di sana?** [siapa di sana?]
Can I smoke here?	**Boleh saya merokok di sini?** [boleh saja meroko' di sini?]
May I ...?	**Boleh saya ...?** [boleh saja ...?]

Needs

I'd like …	**Saya hendak …** [saja henda' …]
I don't want …	**Saya tidak ingin …** [saja tida' iŋin …]
I'm thirsty.	**Saya haus.** [saja haus]
I want to sleep.	**Saya ingin tidur.** [saja iŋin tidur]
I want …	**Saya ingin …** [saja iŋin …]
to wash up	**mandi** [mandi]
to brush my teeth	**menyikat gigi** [menjikat gigi]
to rest a while	**istirahat sebentar** [istirahat sebentar]
to change my clothes	**ganti pakaian** [ganti pakajan]
to go back to the hotel	**kembali ke hotel** [kembali ke hotel]
to buy …	**membeli …** [membeli …]
to go to …	**pergi ke …** [pergi ke …]
to visit …	**mengunjungi …** [meŋundʒ'uŋi …]
to meet with …	**bertemu dengan …** [bertemu deŋan …]
to make a call	**menelepon** [menelepon]
I'm tired.	**Saya lelah.** [saja lelah]
We are tired.	**Kami lelah.** [kami lelah]
I'm cold.	**Saya kedinginan.** [saja kediŋinan]
I'm hot.	**Saya kepanasan.** [saja kepanasan]
I'm OK.	**Saya baik-baik saja.** [saja bai'-bai' sadʒ'a]

I need to make a call.	**Saya perlu menelepon.** [saja perlu menelepon]
I need to go to the restroom.	**Saya perlu pergi ke kamar kecil.** [saja perlu pergi ke kamar ketʃil]
I have to go.	**Saya harus pergi.** [saja harus pergi]
I have to go now.	**Saya harus pergi sekarang.** [saja harus pergi sekaraŋ]

Asking for directions

Excuse me, …	**Permisi, …** [permisi, …]
Where is …?	**Di mana …?** [di mana …?]
Which way is …?	**Ke manakah arah ke …?** [ke manakah arah ke …?]
Could you help me, please?	**Bisakah Anda menolong saya?** [bisakah anda menoloŋ saja?]
I'm looking for …	**Saya sedang mencari …** [saja sedaŋ mentʃari …]
I'm looking for the exit.	**Saya sedang mencari pintu keluar.** [saja sedaŋ mentʃari pintu keluar]
I'm going to …	**Saya akan pergi ke …** [saja akan pergi ke …]
Am I going the right way to …?	**Benarkah ini jalan ke …?** [benarkah ini dʒʲalan ke …?]
Is it far?	**Apakah tempatnya jauh?** [apakah tempatnja dʒʲauh?]
Can I get there on foot?	**Bisakah saya berjalan kaki ke sana?** [bisakah saja berdʒʲalan kaki ke sana?]
Can you show me on the map?	**Bisakah Anda tunjukkan di peta?** [bisakah anda tundʒʲuʔkan di peta?]
Show me where we are right now.	**Tunjukkan di mana lokasi kita sekarang.** [tundʒʲuʔkan di mana lokasi kita sekaraŋ]
Here	**Di sini** [di sini]
There	**Di sana** [di sana]
This way	**Jalan ini** [dʒʲalan ini]
Turn right.	**Belok kanan.** [beloʔ kanan]
Turn left.	**Belok kiri.** [beloʔ kiri]
first (second, third) turn	**belokan pertama (kedua, ketiga)** [belokan pertama (kedua, ketiga)]
to the right	**ke kanan** [ke kanan]

to the left

ke kiri
[ke kiri]

Go straight ahead.

Lurus terus.
[lurus terus]

Signs

WELCOME!	**SELAMAT DATANG!** [selamat dataŋ!]
ENTRANCE	**MASUK** [masuʔ]
EXIT	**KELUAR** [keluar]
PUSH	**DORONG** [doroŋ]
PULL	**TARIK** [tariʔ]
OPEN	**BUKA** [buka]
CLOSED	**TUTUP** [tutup]
FOR WOMEN	**UNTUK PEREMPUAN** [untuʔ perempuan]
FOR MEN	**UNTUK LAKI-LAKI** [untuʔ laki-laki]
GENTLEMEN, GENTS (m)	**PRIA** [pria]
WOMEN (f)	**WANITA** [wanita]
DISCOUNTS	**DISKON** [diskon]
SALE	**OBRAL** [obral]
FREE	**GRATIS** [gratis]
NEW!	**BARU!** [baru!]
ATTENTION!	**PERHATIAN!** [perhatian!]
NO VACANCIES	**KAMAR PENUH** [kamar penuh]
RESERVED	**DIPESAN** [dipesan]
ADMINISTRATION	**ADMINISTRASI** [administrasi]
STAFF ONLY	**HANYA UNTUK STAF** [hanja untuʔ staf]

BEWARE OF THE DOG!	**AWAS ANJING GALAK!** [awas anʤiŋ galaʔ!]
NO SMOKING!	**DILARANG MEROKOK!** [dilaraŋ merokoʔ!]
DO NOT TOUCH!	**JANGAN SENTUH!** [ʤˈaŋan sentuh!]
DANGEROUS	**BERBAHAYA** [berbahaja]
DANGER	**BAHAYA** [bahaja]
HIGH VOLTAGE	**TEGANGAN TINGGI** [tegaŋan tiŋgi]
NO SWIMMING!	**DILARANG BERENANG!** [dilaraŋ berenaŋ!]

OUT OF ORDER	**TIDAK DAPAT DIGUNAKAN** [tidaʔ dapat digunakan]
FLAMMABLE	**MUDAH TERBAKAR** [mudah terbakar]
FORBIDDEN	**DILARANG** [dilaraŋ]
NO TRESPASSING!	**DILARANG MASUK!** [dilaraŋ masuʔ!]
WET PAINT	**CAT BASAH** [ʧat basah]

CLOSED FOR RENOVATIONS	**DITUTUP KARENA ADA PERBAIKAN** [ditutup karena ada perbaikan]
WORKS AHEAD	**ADA PROYEK DI DEPAN** [ada projeʔ di depan]
DETOUR	**JALUR ALTERNATIF** [ʤˈalur alternatif]

Transportation. General phrases

plane	**pesawat** [pesawat]
train	**kereta api** [kereta api]
bus	**bus** [bus]
ferry	**feri** [feri]
taxi	**taksi** [taksi]
car	**mobil** [mobil]
schedule	**jadwal** [dʒadwal]
Where can I see the schedule?	**Di mana saya dapat melihat jadwalnya?** [di mana saja dapat melihat dʒadwalnja?]
workdays (weekdays)	**hari kerja** [hari kerdʒa]
weekends	**akhir pekan** [ahir pekan]
holidays	**hari libur** [hari libur]
DEPARTURE	**KEBERANGKATAN** [keberaŋkatan]
ARRIVAL	**KEDATANGAN** [kedataŋan]
DELAYED	**DITUNDA** [ditunda]
CANCELLED	**DIBATALKAN** [dibatalkan]
next (train, etc.)	**berikutnya** [berikutnja]
first	**pertama** [pertama]
last	**terakhir** [terahir]

When is the next ...?	**Kapan ... berikutnya?** [kapan ... berikutnja?]
When is the first ...?	**Kapan ... pertama?** [kapan ... pertama?]
When is the last ...?	**Kapan ... terakhir?** [kapan ... terahir?]

transfer (change of trains, etc.)	**pindah** [pindah]
to make a transfer	**berpindah** [berpindah]
Do I need to make a transfer?	**Haruskah saya berpindah?** [haruskah saja berpindah?]

Buying tickets

Where can I buy tickets?	**Di mana saya dapat membeli tiket?** [di mana saja dapat membeli tiket?]
ticket	**tiket** [tiket]
to buy a ticket	**membeli tiket** [membeli tiket]
ticket price	**harga tiket** [harga tiket]
Where to?	**Ke mana?** [ke mana?]
To what station?	**Ke stasiun apa?** [ke stasiun apa?]
I need ...	**Saya perlu ...** [saja perlu ...]
one ticket	**satu tiket** [satu tiket]
two tickets	**dua tiket** [dua tiket]
three tickets	**tiga tiket** [tiga tiket]
one-way	**sekali jalan** [sekali ʤʲalan]
round-trip	**pulang pergi** [pulaŋ pergi]
first class	**kelas satu** [kelas satu]
second class	**kelas dua** [kelas dua]
today	**hari ini** [hari ini]
tomorrow	**besok** [besoʔ]
the day after tomorrow	**lusa** [lusa]
in the morning	**pagi** [pagi]
in the afternoon	**siang** [siaŋ]
in the evening	**malam** [malam]

aisle seat

kursi dekat lorong
[kursi dekat loroŋ]

window seat

kursi dekat jendela
[kursi dekat ʤʲendela]

How much?

Berapa harganya?
[berapa harganja?]

Can I pay by credit card?

Bisakah saya membayar dengan kartu kredit?
[bisakah saja membajar deŋan kartu kredit?]

Bus

bus	**bus** [bus]
intercity bus	**bus antarkota** [bus antarkota]
bus stop	**pemberhentian bus** [pemberhentian bus]
Where's the nearest bus stop?	**Di mana pemberhentian bus terdekat?** [di mana pemberhentian bus terdekat?]
number (bus ~, etc.)	**nomor** [nomor]
Which bus do I take to get to ...?	**Bus apa yang ke ...?** [bus apa jaŋ ke ...?]
Does this bus go to ...?	**Apakah bus ini ke ...?** [apakah bus ini ke ...?]
How frequent are the buses?	**Seberapa sering busnya datang?** [seberapa seriŋ busnja dataŋ?]
every 15 minutes	**setiap 15 menit** [setiap lima belas menit]
every half hour	**setiap setengah jam** [setiap seteŋah dʒˈam]
every hour	**setiap jam** [setiap dʒˈam]
several times a day	**beberapa kali sehari** [beberapa kali sehari]
... times a day	**... kali sehari** [... kali sehari]
schedule	**jadwal** [dʒˈadwal]
Where can I see the schedule?	**Di mana saya dapat melihat jadwalnya?** [di mana saja dapat melihat dʒˈadwalnja?]
When is the next bus?	**Kapan bus berikutnya?** [kapan bus berikutnja?]
When is the first bus?	**Kapan bus pertama?** [kapan bus pertama?]
When is the last bus?	**Kapan bus terakhir?** [kapan bus terahir?]

stop

pemberhentian
[pemberhentian]

next stop

pemberhentian berikutnya
[pemberhentian berikutnja]

last stop (terminus)

pemberhentian terakhir (terminal)
[pemberhentian terahir (terminal)]

Stop here, please.

Berhenti di sini.
[berhenti di sini]

Excuse me, this is my stop.

Permisi, saya turun di sini.
[permisi, saja turun di sini]

Train

train	**kereta api** [kereta api]
suburban train	**kereta api lokal** [kereta api lokal]
long-distance train	**kereta api jarak jauh** [kereta api ʤarak ʤauh]
train station	**stasiun kereta api** [stasiun kereta api]
Excuse me, where is the exit to the platform?	**Permisi, di manakah pintu ke arah peron?** [permisi, di manakah pintu ke arah peron?]
Does this train go to ...?	**Apakah kereta api ini menuju ke ...?** [apakah kereta api ini menuʤu ke ...?]
next train	**kereta api berikutnya** [kereta api berikutnja]
When is the next train?	**Kapan kereta api berikutnya?** [kapan kereta api berikutnja?]
Where can I see the schedule?	**Di mana saya dapat melihat jadwalnya?** [di mana saja dapat melihat ʤadwalnja?]
From which platform?	**Dari peron jalur berapa?** [dari peron ʤalur berapa?]
When does the train arrive in ...?	**Kapan kereta api ini sampai di ...?** [kapan kereta api ini sampaj di ...?]
Please help me.	**Tolong bantu saya.** [toloŋ bantu saja]
I'm looking for my seat.	**Saya sedang mencari kursi saya.** [saja sedaŋ mentʃari kursi saja]
We're looking for our seats.	**Kami sedang mencari kursi kami.** [kami sedaŋ mentʃari kursi kami]
My seat is taken.	**Kursi saya sudah ditempati.** [kursi saja sudah ditempati]
Our seats are taken.	**Kursi kami sudah ditempati.** [kursi kami sudah ditempati]
I'm sorry but this is my seat.	**Maaf, ini kursi saya.** [maʔaf, ini kursi saja]

Is this seat taken? **Apakah kursi ini sudah diambil?**
[apakah kursi ini sudah diambil?]

May I sit here? **Boleh saya duduk di sini?**
[boleh saja dudu' di sini?]

On the train. Dialogue (No ticket)

Ticket, please.

Permisi, tiketnya.
[permisi, tiketnja]

I don't have a ticket.

Saya tidak punya tiket.
[saja tida' punja tiket]

I lost my ticket.

Tiket saya hilang.
[tiket saja hilaŋ]

I forgot my ticket at home.

Tiket saya tertinggal di rumah.
[tiket saja tertiŋgal di rumah]

You can buy a ticket from me.

Anda bisa membeli tiket dari saya.
[anda bisa membeli tiket dari saja]

You will also have to pay a fine.

Anda juga harus membayar denda.
[anda dʒuga harus membajar denda]

Okay.

Baik.
[bai']

Where are you going?

Ke manakah tujuan Anda?
[ke manakah tudʒuan anda?]

I'm going to …

Saya akan pergi ke …
[saja akan pergi ke …]

How much? I don't understand.

Berapa harganya? Saya tidak mengerti.
[berapa harganja? saja tida' meŋerti]

Write it down, please.

Tolong tuliskan.
[toloŋ tuliskan]

Okay. Can I pay with a credit card?

Baik. Bisakah saya membayar dengan kartu kredit?
[bai'. bisakah saja membajar deŋan kartu kredit?]

Yes, you can.

Ya, bisa.
[ja, bisa]

Here's your receipt.

Ini tanda terimanya.
[ini tanda terimanja]

Sorry about the fine.

Maaf atas dendanya.
[ma'af atas dendanja]

That's okay. It was my fault.

Tidak apa-apa. Saya yang salah.
[tida' apa-apa. saja jaŋ salah.]

Enjoy your trip.

Selamat menikmati perjalanan.
[selamat menikmati perdʒalanan]

Taxi

taxi

taksi
[taksi]

taxi driver

sopir taksi
[sopir taksi]

to catch a taxi

menyetop taksi
[menjetop taksi]

taxi stand

pangkalan taksi
[paŋkalan taksi]

Where can I get a taxi?

Di mana saya bisa mendapatkan taksi?
[di mana saja bisa mendapatkan taksi?]

to call a taxi

menelepon taksi
[menelepon taksi]

I need a taxi.

Saya perlu taksi.
[saja perlu taksi]

Right now.

Sekarang.
[sekaraŋ]

What is your address (location)?

Di mana alamat Anda?
[di mana alamat anda?]

My address is ...

Alamat saya di ...
[alamat saja di ...]

Your destination?

Tujuan Anda?
[tudʒiuan anda?]

Excuse me, ...

Permisi, ...
[permisi, ...]

Are you available?

Apa taksi ini kosong?
[apa taksi ini kosoŋ?]

How much is it to get to ...?

Berapa ongkos ke ...?
[berapa oŋkos ke ...?]

Do you know where it is?

Tahukah Anda tempatnya?
[tahukah anda tempatnja?]

Airport, please.

Ke bandara.
[ke bandara]

Stop here, please.

Berhenti di sini.
[berhenti di sini]

It's not here.

Bukan di sini.
[bukan di sini]

This is the wrong address.

Alamatnya salah.
[alamatnja salah]

Turn left.	**Belok kiri** [belo' kiri]
Turn right.	**Belok kanan.** [belo' kanan]

How much do I owe you?	**Berapa yang harus saya bayar?** [berapa jaŋ harus saja bajar?]
I'd like a receipt, please.	**Saya minta tanda terimanya.** [saja minta tanda terimanja]
Keep the change.	**Kembaliannya untuk Anda.** [kembaliannja untu' anda]

Would you please wait for me?	**Maukah Anda menunggu saya?** [maukah anda menuŋgu saja?]
five minutes	**lima menit** [lima menit]
ten minutes	**sepuluh menit** [sepuluh menit]
fifteen minutes	**lima belas menit** [lima belas menit]
twenty minutes	**dua puluh menit** [dua puluh menit]
half an hour	**setengah jam** [seteŋah ʤ'am]

Hotel

Hello.	**Halo.** [halo]
My name is …	**Nama saya ...** [nama saja ...]
I have a reservation.	**Saya sudah memesan.** [saja sudah memesan]
I need …	**Saya perlu ...** [saja perlu ...]
a single room	**kamar single** [kamar siŋle]
a double room	**kamar double** [kamar double]
How much is that?	**Berapa harganya?** [berapa harganja?]
That's a bit expensive.	**Agak mahal.** [aga’ mahal]
Do you have anything else?	**Apa Anda punya opsi lain?** [apa anda punja opsi lain?]
I'll take it.	**Saya ambil.** [saja ambil]
I'll pay in cash.	**Saya bayar tunai.** [saja bajar tunaj]
I've got a problem.	**Saya sedang kesulitan.** [saja sedaŋ kesulitan]
My … is broken.	**... saya rusak.** [... saja rusa’]
My … is out of order.	**... saya tidak dapat digunakan.** [... saja tida’ dapat digunakan]
TV	**TV** [tv]
air conditioner	**alat pendingin hawa** [alat pendiŋin hawa]
tap	**keran** [keran]
shower	**pancuran** [pantʃuran]
sink	**bak cuci** [ba’ tʃutʃi]
safe	**brankas** [brankas]

door lock	**kunci pintu** [kuntʃi pintu]
electrical outlet	**stopkontak** [stopkontak]
hairdryer	**pegering rambut** [pegeriŋ rambut]

I don't have …	**Tidak ada …** [tidaʔ ada …]
water	**air** [air]
light	**lampu** [lampu]
electricity	**listrik** [listriʔ]

Can you give me …?	**Bisakah Anda memberi saya …?** [bisakah anda memberi saja …?]
a towel	**handuk** [handuʔ]
a blanket	**selimut** [selimut]
slippers	**sandal** [sandal]
a robe	**jubah** [dʒʲubah]
shampoo	**sampo** [sampo]
soap	**sabun** [sabun]

I'd like to change rooms.	**Saya ingin pindah kamar.** [saja iŋin pindah kamar]
I can't find my key.	**Kunci saya tidak ketemu.** [kuntʃi saja tidaʔ ketemu]
Could you open my room, please?	**Bisakah Anda membukakan pintu saya?** [bisakah anda membukakan pintu saja?]

Who's there?	**Siapa di sana?** [siapa di sana?]
Come in!	**Masuk!** [masuʔ!]
Just a minute!	**Tunggu sebentar!** [tuŋgu sebentar!]

Not right now, please.	**Jangan sekarang.** [dʒʲaŋan sekaraŋ]
Come to my room, please.	**Datanglah ke kamar saya.** [dataŋlah ke kamar saja]

I'd like to order food service.

Saya ingin memesan makanan.
[saja injin memesan makanan]

My room number is …

Nomor kamar saya ...
[nomor kamar saja ...]

I'm leaving …

Saya pergi ...
[saja pergi ...]

We're leaving …

Kami pergi ...
[kami pergi ...]

right now

sekarang
[sekaran]

this afternoon

siang ini
[sian ini]

tonight

malam ini
[malam ini]

tomorrow

besok
[beso']

tomorrow morning

besok pagi
[beso' pagi]

tomorrow evening

besok malam
[beso' malam]

the day after tomorrow

lusa
[lusa]

I'd like to pay.

Saya hendak membayar.
[saja henda' membajar]

Everything was wonderful.

Segalanya luar biasa.
[segalanja luar biasa]

Where can I get a taxi?

Di mana saya bisa mendapatkan taksi?
[di mana saja bisa mendapatkan taksi?]

Would you call a taxi for me, please?

Bisakah Anda memanggilkan saya taksi?
[bisakah anda memangilkan saja taksi?]

Restaurant

Can I look at the menu, please?
Bisakah saya melihat menunya?
[bisakah saja melihat menunja?]

Table for one.
Meja untuk satu orang.
[medʒ'a untu' satu oraŋ]

There are two (three, four) of us.
Kami berdua (bertiga, berempat).
[kami berdua (bertiga, berempat)]

Smoking
Ruang Merokok
[ruaŋ meroko']

No smoking
Ruang Bebas Rokok
[ruaŋ bebas roko']

Excuse me! (addressing a waiter)
Permisi!
[permisi!]

menu
menu
[menu]

wine list
daftar anggur
[daftar aŋgur]

The menu, please.
Tolong menunya.
[toloŋ menunja]

Are you ready to order?
Apakah Anda siap memesan?
[apakah anda siap memesan?]

What will you have?
Apa yang ingin Anda pesan?
[apa jaŋ iŋin anda pesan?]

I'll have …
Saya ingin memesan …
[saja iŋin memesan …]

I'm a vegetarian.
Saya vegetarian.
[saja vegetarian]

meat
daging
[dagiŋ]

fish
ikan
[ikan]

vegetables
sayur mayur
[sajur majur]

Do you have vegetarian dishes?
Apa Anda punya hidangan vegetarian?
[apa anda punja hidaŋan vegetarian?]

I don't eat pork.
Saya tidak makan daging babi.
[saja tida' makan dagiŋ babi]

He /she/ doesn't eat meat.
Dia tidak makan daging.
[dia tida' makan dagiŋ]

I am allergic to …

Saya alergi …
[saja alergi …]

Would you please bring me …

Tolong ambilkan …
[toloŋ ambilkan …]

salt | pepper | sugar

garam | merica | gula
[garam | meritʃa | gula]

coffee | tea | dessert

kopi | teh | pencuci mulut
[kopi | teh | pentʃutʃi mulut]

water | sparkling | plain

air | air soda | air putih
[air | air soda | air putih]

a spoon | fork | knife

sendok | garpu | pisau
[sendoʼ | garpu | pisau]

a plate | napkin

piring | serbet
[piriŋ | serbet]

Enjoy your meal!

Selamat menikmati!
[selamat menikmati!]

One more, please.

Tambah satu lagi.
[tambah satu lagi]

It was very delicious.

Benar-benar lezat.
[benar-benar lezat]

check | change | tip

tagihan | kembalian | tip
[tagihan | kembalian | tip]

Check, please.
(Could I have the check, please?)

Tolong tagihannya.
[toloŋ tagihannja]

Can I pay by credit card?

Bisakah saya membayar dengan kartu kredit?
[bisakah saja membajar deŋan kartu kredit?]

I'm sorry, there's a mistake here.

Maaf, ada kesalahan di sini.
[maʼaf, ada kesalahan di sini]

Shopping

Can I help you?	**Ada yang bisa saya bantu?** [ada jaŋ bisa saja bantu?]
Do you have …?	**Apa Anda punya ...?** [apa anda punja ...?]
I'm looking for …	**Saya sedang mencari ...** [saja sedaŋ mentʃari ...]
I need …	**Saya perlu ...** [saja perlu ...]
I'm just looking.	**Saya hanya melihat-lihat.** [saja hanja melihat-lihat]
We're just looking.	**Kami hanya melihat-lihat.** [kami hanja melihat-lihat]
I'll come back later.	**Saya akan kembali lagi nanti.** [saja akan kembali lagi nanti]
We'll come back later.	**Kami akan kembali lagi nanti.** [kami akan kembali lagi nanti]
discounts | sale	**diskon | obral** [diskon | obral]
Would you please show me …	**Bisakah Anda tunjukkan ...** [bisakah anda tundʒuʔkan ...]
Would you please give me …	**Bisakah Anda ambilkan ...** [bisakah anda ambilkan ...]
Can I try it on?	**Bisakah saya mencobanya?** [bisakah saja mentʃobanja?]
Excuse me, where's the fitting room?	**Permisi, di mana kamar pasnya?** [permisi, di mana kamar pasnja?]
Which color would you like?	**Warna apa yang Anda inginkan?** [warna apa jaŋ anda iŋinkan?]
size | length	**ukuran | panjang** [ukuran | pandʒʲaŋ]
How does it fit?	**Apakah pas?** [apakah pas?]
How much is it?	**Berapa harganya?** [berapa harganja?]
That's too expensive.	**Itu terlalu mahal.** [itu terlalu mahal]
I'll take it.	**Saya ambil.** [saja ambil]
Excuse me, where do I pay?	**Permisi, di mana saya harus membayar?** [permisi, di mana saja harus membajar?]

Will you pay in cash or credit card?

Apakah Anda ingin membayar tunai atau dengan kartu kredit?
[apakah anda iŋin membajar tunaj atau deŋan kartu kredit?]

In cash | with credit card

Tunai | dengan kartu kredit
[tunaj | deŋan kartu kredit]

Do you want the receipt?

Apakah Anda ingin tanda terimanya?
[apakah anda iŋin tanda terimanja?]

Yes, please.

Ya.
[ja]

No, it's OK.

Tidak, tidak usah.
[tidaʔ, tidaʔ usah]

Thank you. Have a nice day!

Terima kasih. Semoga hari Anda menyenangkan!
[terima kasih. semoga hari anda menjenaŋkan!]

In town

Excuse me, please.	**Permisi, ...** [permisi, …]
I'm looking for …	**Saya sedang mencari ...** [saja sedaŋ mentʃari ...]
the subway	**stasiun bawah tanah** [stasiun bawah tanah]
my hotel	**hotel saya** [hotel saja]
the movie theater	**bioskop** [bioskop]
a taxi stand	**pangkalan taksi** [paŋkalan taksi]
an ATM	**ATM** [a-te-em]
a foreign exchange office	**tempat penukaran mata uang** [tempat penukaran mata uaŋ]
an internet café	**warnet** [warnet]
… street	**Jalan ...** [dʒʲalan ...]
this place	**tempat ini** [tempat ini]
Do you know where … is?	**Apakah Anda tahu lokasi ...?** [apakah anda tahu lokasi ...?]
Which street is this?	**Jalan apakah ini?** [dʒʲalan apakah ini?]
Show me where we are right now.	**Tunjukkan di mana lokasi kita sekarang.** [tundʒiuʔkan di mana lokasi kita sekaraŋ]
Can I get there on foot?	**Bisakah saya berjalan kaki ke sana?** [bisakah saja berdʒʲalan kaki ke sana?]
Do you have a map of the city?	**Apa Anda punya peta kota?** [apa anda punja peta kota?]
How much is a ticket to get in?	**Berapa harga tiket masuk?** [berapa harga tiket masuʔ?]
Can I take pictures here?	**Bisakah saya berfoto di sini?** [bisakah saja berfoto di sini?]
Are you open?	**Apakah Anda buka?** [apakah anda buka?]

When do you open?

Kapan Anda buka?
[kapan anda buka?]

When do you close?

Kapan Anda tutup?
[kapan anda tutup?]

Money

money	**uang** [uaŋ]
cash	**tunai** [tunaj]
paper money	**uang kertas** [uaŋ kertas]
loose change	**uang receh** [uaŋ retʃeh]
check | change | tip	**tagihan | kembalian | tip** [tagihan | kembalian | tip]
credit card	**kartu kredit** [kartu kredit]
wallet	**dompet** [dompet]
to buy	**membeli** [membeli]
to pay	**membayar** [membajar]
fine	**denda** [denda]
free	**gratis** [gratis]
Where can I buy ...?	**Di mana saya bisa membeli ...?** [di mana saja bisa membeli ...?]
Is the bank open now?	**Apakah bank buka sekarang?** [apakah banʔ buka sekaraŋ?]
When does it open?	**Kapan bank buka?** [kapan bank buka?]
When does it close?	**Kapan bank tutup?** [kapan bank tutup?]
How much?	**Berapa harganya?** [berapa harganja?]
How much is this?	**Berapa harganya?** [berapa harganja?]
That's too expensive.	**Itu terlalu mahal.** [itu terlalu mahal]
Excuse me, where do I pay?	**Permisi, di mana saya harus membayar?** [permisi, di mana saja harus membajar?]

Check, please.

Tolong tagihannya.
[toloŋ tagihannja]

Can I pay by credit card?

Bisakah saya membayar dengan kartu kredit?
[bisakah saja membajar deŋan kartu kredit?]

Is there an ATM here?

Adakah ATM di sini?
[adakah a-te-em di sini?]

I'm looking for an ATM.

Saya sedang mencari ATM.
[saja sedaŋ mentʃari a-te-em]

I'm looking for a foreign exchange office.

Saya sedang mencari tempat penukaran mata uang.
[saja sedaŋ mentʃari tempat penukaran mata uaŋ]

I'd like to change …

Saya ingin menukarkan …
[saja iŋin menukarkan …]

What is the exchange rate?

Berapakah nilai tukarnya?
[berapakah nilaj tukarnja?]

Do you need my passport?

Apa Anda butuh paspor saya?
[apa anda butuh paspor saja?]

Time

What time is it?	**Jam berapa sekarang?** [dʒ'am berapa sekaraŋ?]
When?	**Kapan?** [kapan?]
At what time?	**Jam berapa?** [dʒ'am berapa?]
now | later | after ...	**sekarang | nanti | setelah ...** [sekaraŋ | nanti | setelah ...]
one o'clock	**pukul satu** [pukul satu]
one fifteen	**pukul satu lewat lima belas** [pukul satu lewat lima belas]
one thirty	**pukul satu lewat tiga puluh** [pukul satu lewat tiga puluh]
one forty-five	**pukul satu lewat empat puluh lima** [pukul satu lewat empat puluh lima]
one | two | three	**satu | dua | tiga** [satu | dua | tiga]
four | five | six	**empat | lima | enam** [empat | lima | enam]
seven | eight | nine	**tujuh | delapan | sembilan** [tudʒ'uh | delapan | sembilan]
ten | eleven | twelve	**sepuluh | sebelas | dua belas** [sepuluh | sebelas | dua belas]
in ...	**dalam ...** [dalam ...]
five minutes	**lima menit** [lima menit]
ten minutes	**sepuluh menit** [sepuluh menit]
fifteen minutes	**lima belas menit** [lima belas menit]
twenty minutes	**dua puluh menit** [dua puluh menit]
half an hour	**setengah jam** [seteŋah dʒ'am]
an hour	**satu jam** [satu dʒ'am]
in the morning	**pagi** [pagi]
early in the morning	**pagi-pagi sekali** [pagi-pagi sekali]

this morning	**pagi ini** [pagi ini]
tomorrow morning	**besok pagi** [beso' pagi]
in the middle of the day	**tengah hari** [teŋah hari]
in the afternoon	**siang** [siaŋ]
in the evening	**malam** [malam]
tonight	**malam ini** [malam ini]
at night	**pada malam hari** [pada malam hari]
yesterday	**kemarin** [kemarin]
today	**hari ini** [hari ini]
tomorrow	**besok** [beso']
the day after tomorrow	**lusa** [lusa]
What day is it today?	**Hari apa sekarang?** [hari apa sekaraŋ?]
It's ...	**Sekarang ...** [sekaraŋ ...]
Monday	**Hari Senin** [hari senin]
Tuesday	**Hari Selasa** [hari selasa]
Wednesday	**Hari Rabu** [hari rabu]
Thursday	**Hari Kamis** [hari kamis]
Friday	**Hari Jumat** [hari dʒ'umat]
Saturday	**Hari Sabtu** [hari sabtu]
Sunday	**Hari Minggu** [hari miŋgu]

Greetings. Introductions

Hello.	**Halo.** [halo]
Pleased to meet you.	**Senang dapat berjumpa dengan Anda.** [senaŋ dapat berʤumpa deŋan anda]
Me too.	**Sama-sama.** [sama-sama]
I'd like you to meet ...	**Kenalkan, ...** [kenalkan, ...]
Nice to meet you.	**Senang dapat berjumpa dengan Anda.** [senaŋ dapat berʤumpa deŋan anda]
How are you?	**Apa kabar?** [apa kabar?]
My name is ...	**Nama saya ...** [nama saja ...]
His name is ...	**Namanya ...** [namanja ...]
Her name is ...	**Namanya ...** [namanja ...]
What's your name?	**Siapa nama Anda?** [siapa nama anda?]
What's his name?	**Siapa namanya?** [siapa namanja?]
What's her name?	**Siapa namanya?** [siapa namanja?]
What's your last name?	**Siapa nama belakang Anda?** [siapa nama belakaŋ anda?]
You can call me ...	**Panggil saya ...** [paŋgil saja ...]
Where are you from?	**Dari mana asal Anda?** [dari mana asal anda?]
I'm from ...	**Saya dari ...** [saja dari ...]
What do you do for a living?	**Apa pekerjaan Anda?** [apa pekerʤa'an anda?]
Who is this?	**Siapa ini?** [siapa ini?]
Who is he?	**Siapa dia?** [siapa dia?]
Who is she?	**Siapa dia?** [siapa dia?]

Who are they?	**Siapa mereka?** [siapa mereka?]
This is ...	**Ini ...** [ini ...]
my friend (masc.)	**teman saya** [teman saja]
my friend (fem.)	**teman saya** [teman saja]
my husband	**suami saya** [suami saja]
my wife	**istri saya** [istri saja]
my father	**ayah saya** [ajah saja]
my mother	**ibu saya** [ibu saja]
my brother	**saudara laki-laki saya** [saudara laki-laki saja]
my sister	**saudara perempuan saya** [saudara perempuan saja]
my son	**anak laki-laki saya** [ana' laki-laki saja]
my daughter	**anak perempuan saya** [ana' perempuan saja]
This is our son.	**Ini anak laki-laki kami.** [ini ana' laki-laki kami]
This is our daughter.	**Ini anak perempuan kami.** [ini ana' perempuan kami]
These are my children.	**Ini anak-anak saya.** [ini ana'-ana' saja]
These are our children.	**Ini anak-anak kami.** [ini ana'-ana' kami]

Farewells

Good bye!	**Selamat tinggal!** [selamat tiŋgal!]
Bye! (inform.)	**Dadah!** [dadah!]
See you tomorrow.	**Sampai bertemu besok.** [sampaj bertemu beso?]
See you soon.	**Sampai jumpa.** [sampaj dʒi umpa]
See you at seven.	**Sampai jumpa pukul tujuh.** [sampaj dʒi umpa pukul tudʒi uh]
Have fun!	**Selamat bersenang-senang!** [selamat bersenaŋ-senaŋ!]
Talk to you later.	**Kita mengobrol lagi nanti.** [kita meŋobrol lagi nanti]
Have a nice weekend.	**Selamat berakhir pekan.** [selamat berahir pekan]
Good night.	**Selamat malam.** [selamat malam]
It's time for me to go.	**Sudah waktunya saya pamit.** [sudah waktunja saja pamit]
I have to go.	**Saya harus pergi.** [saja harus pergi]
I will be right back.	**Saya akan segera kembali.** [saja akan segera kembali]
It's late.	**Sudah larut.** [sudah larut]
I have to get up early.	**Saya harus bangun pagi.** [saja harus baŋun pagi]
I'm leaving tomorrow.	**Saya pergi besok.** [saja pergi beso?]
We're leaving tomorrow.	**Kami pergi besok.** [kami pergi beso?]
Have a nice trip!	**Semoga perjalanan Anda menyenangkan!** [semoga perdʒi alanan anda menjenaŋkan!]
It was nice meeting you.	**Senang dapat berjumpa dengan Anda.** [senaŋ dapat berdʒi umpa deŋan anda]

It was nice talking to you.
Senang dapat berbincang dengan Anda.
[senaŋ dapat berbintʃaŋ deŋan anda]

Thanks for everything.
Terima kasih atas segalanya.
[terima kasih atas segalanja]

I had a very good time.
Saya senang sekali hari ini.
[saja senaŋ sekali hari ini]

We had a very good time.
Kami senang sekali hari ini.
[kami senaŋ sekali hari ini]

It was really great.
Hari yang luar biasa.
[hari jaŋ luar biasa]

I'm going to miss you.
Saya akan merindukan Anda.
[saja akan merindukan anda]

We're going to miss you.
Kami akan merindukan Anda.
[kami akan merindukan anda]

Good luck!
Semoga berhasil!
[semoga berhasil!]

Say hi to …
Sampaikan salam saya untuk ...
[sampajkan salam saja untu' ...]

Foreign language

I don't understand.	**Saya tidak mengerti.** [saja tida' meŋerti]
Write it down, please.	**Tolong tuliskan.** [toloŋ tuliskan]
Do you speak ...?	**Apa Anda bisa berbahasa ...?** [apa anda bisa berbahasa ...?]
I speak a little bit of ...	**Saya bisa sedikit berbahasa ...** [saja bisa sedikit berbahasa ...]
English	**Inggris** [iŋgris]
Turkish	**Turki** [turki]
Arabic	**Arab** [arab]
French	**Perancis** [perantʃis]
German	**Jerman** [dʒˈerman]
Italian	**Italia** [italia]
Spanish	**Spanyol** [spanjol]
Portuguese	**Portugis** [portugis]
Chinese	**Mandarin** [mandarin]
Japanese	**Jepang** [dʒˈepaŋ]
Can you repeat that, please.	**Bisakah Anda mengulanginya?** [bisakah anda meŋulaŋinja?]
I understand.	**Saya mengerti.** [saja meŋerti]
I don't understand.	**Saya tidak mengerti.** [saja tida' meŋerti]
Please speak more slowly.	**Tolong berbicara lebih lambat.** [toloŋ berbitʃara lebih lambat]
Is that correct? (Am I saying it right?)	**Apakah itu benar?** [apakah itu benar?]
What is this? (What does this mean?)	**Apa ini? (Apa artinya ini?)** [apa ini? (apa artinja ini?)]

Apologies

Excuse me, please.	**Permisi.**
	[permisi]
I'm sorry.	**Maaf.**
	[ma'af]
I'm really sorry.	**Saya benar-benar minta maaf.**
	[saja benar-benar minta ma'af]
Sorry, it's my fault.	**Maaf, itu kesalahan saya.**
	[ma'af, itu kesalahan saja]
My mistake.	**Saya yang salah.**
	[saja jaŋ salah]

May I ...?	**Boleh saya ...?**
	[boleh saja ...?]
Do you mind if I ...?	**Apakah Anda keberatan jika saya ...?**
	[apakah anda keberatan ʤika saja ...?]
It's OK.	**Tidak apa-apa.**
	[tida' apa-apa]
It's all right.	**Tidak apa-apa.**
	[tida' apa-apa]
Don't worry about it.	**Jangan khawatir.**
	[ʤ'aŋan hawatir]

Agreement

Yes.	**Ya.** [ja]
Yes, sure.	**Ya, tentu saja.** [ja, tentu sadʒ'a]
OK (Good!)	**Bagus!** [bagus!]
Very well.	**Baiklah.** [baiklah]
Certainly!	**Tentu saja.** [tentu sadʒ'a]
I agree.	**Saya setuju.** [saja setudʒ'u]
That's correct.	**Betul.** [betul]
That's right.	**Benar.** [benar]
You're right.	**Anda benar.** [anda benar]
I don't mind.	**Saya tidak keberatan.** [saja tidak keberatan]
Absolutely right.	**Benar sekali.** [benar sekali]
It's possible.	**Mungkin saja.** [muŋkin sadʒ'a]
That's a good idea.	**Ide bagus.** [ide bagus]
I can't say no.	**Saya tidak bisa menolaknya.** [saja tida' bisa menolaknja]
I'd be happy to.	**Dengan senang hati.** [deŋan senaŋ hati]
With pleasure.	**Dengan senang hati.** [deŋan senaŋ hati]

Refusal. Expressing doubt

No.	**Tidak.** [tida?]
Certainly not.	**Tentu saja tidak.** [tentu sadʒia tida?]
I don't agree.	**Saya tidak setuju.** [saja tida? setudʒiu]
I don't think so.	**Saya rasa tidak begitu.** [saja rasa tida? begitu]
It's not true.	**Tidak benar.** [tida? benar]
You are wrong.	**Anda keliru.** [anda keliru]
I think you are wrong.	**Saya rasa Anda keliru.** [saja rasa anda keliru]
I'm not sure.	**Saya kurang yakin.** [saja kuraŋ jakin]
It's impossible.	**Tidak mungkin.** [tida? muŋkin]
Nothing of the kind (sort)!	**Itu mengada-ada!** [itu meŋada-ada!]
The exact opposite.	**Justru kebalikannya.** [dʒiustru kebalikannja]
I'm against it.	**Saya menentangnya.** [saja menentaŋnja]
I don't care.	**Saya tidak peduli.** [saja tida? peduli]
I have no idea.	**Saya tidak tahu.** [saja tida? tahu]
I doubt it.	**Saya meragukannya.** [saja meragukannja]
Sorry, I can't.	**Maaf, saya tidak bisa.** [ma?af, saja tida? bisa]
Sorry, I don't want to.	**Maaf, saya tidak mau.** [ma?af, saja tida? mau]
Thank you, but I don't need this.	**Maaf, saya tidak membutuhkannya.** [ma?af, saja tida? membutuhkannja]
It's getting late.	**Sudah semakin larut.** [sudah semakin larut]

I have to get up early.

Saya harus bangun pagi.
[saja harus baŋun pagi]

I don't feel well.

Saya tidak enak badan.
[saja tida' enak badan]

Expressing gratitude

Thank you.	**Terima kasih.** [terima kasih]
Thank you very much.	**Terima kasih banyak.** [terima kasih banjaʔ]
I really appreciate it.	**Saya sangat menghargainya.** [saja saŋat meŋhargainja]
I'm really grateful to you.	**Saya sangat berterima kasih kepada Anda.** [saja saŋat berterima kasih kepada anda]
We are really grateful to you.	**Kami sangat berterima kasih kepada Anda.** [kami saŋat berterima kasih kepada anda]

Thank you for your time.	**Terima kasih atas waktu Anda.** [terima kasih atas waktu anda]
Thanks for everything.	**Terima kasih atas segalanya.** [terima kasih atas segalanja]
Thank you for …	**Terima kasih atas ...** [terima kasih atas ...]
your help	**bantuan Anda** [bantuan anda]
a nice time	**saat yang menyenangkan ini** [saʔat jaŋ menjenaŋkan ini]

a wonderful meal	**hidangan yang luar biasa ini** [hidaŋan jaŋ luar biasa ini]
a pleasant evening	**malam yang menyenangkan ini** [malam jaŋ menjenaŋkan ini]
a wonderful day	**hari yang luar biasa ini** [hari jaŋ luar biasa ini]
an amazing journey	**perjalanan yang menakjubkan ini** [perdʒalanan jaŋ menakdʒubkan ini]

Don't mention it.	**Jangan sungkan.** [dʒaŋan suŋkan]
You are welcome.	**Terima kasih kembali.** [terima kasih kembali]
Any time.	**Sama-sama.** [sama-sama]
My pleasure.	**Dengan senang hati.** [deŋan senaŋ hati]

Forget it.   **Jangan sungkan.**
                                    [dʒˈaŋan suŋkan]

Don't worry about it.   **Jangan khawatir.**
                                    [dʒˈaŋan hawatir]

Congratulations. Best wishes

Congratulations!	**Selamat!** [selamat!]
Happy birthday!	**Selamat ulang tahun!** [selamat ulaŋ tahun!]
Merry Christmas!	**Selamat Natal!** [selamat natal!]
Happy New Year!	**Selamat Tahun Baru!** [selamat tahun baru!]
Happy Easter!	**Selamat Paskah!** [selamat paskah!]
Happy Hanukkah!	**Selamat Hanukkah!** [selamat hanuʔkah!]
I'd like to propose a toast.	**Saya ingin bersulang.** [saja iŋin bersulaŋ]
Cheers!	**Bersulang!** [bersulaŋ!]
Let's drink to ...!	**Mari bersulang demi ...!** [mari bersulaŋ demi ...!]
To our success!	**Demi keberhasilan kita!** [demi keberhasilan kita!]
To your success!	**Demi keberhasilan Anda!** [demi keberhasilan anda!]
Good luck!	**Semoga berhasil!** [semoga berhasil!]
Have a nice day!	**Semoga hari Anda menyenangkan!** [semoga hari anda menjenaŋkan!]
Have a good holiday!	**Selamat berlibur!** [selamat berlibur!]
Have a safe journey!	**Semoga perjalanan Anda menyenangkan!** [semoga perdʒalanan anda menjenaŋkan!]
I hope you get better soon!	**Semoga cepat sembuh!** [semoga tʃepat sembuh!]

Socializing

Why are you sad?	**Mengapa Anda sedih?** [meŋapa anda sedih?]
Smile! Cheer up!	**Tersenyumlah! Bersemangatlah!** [tersenjumlah! bersemaŋatlah!]
Are you free tonight?	**Apa Anda punya waktu malam ini?** [apa anda punja waktu malam ini?]
May I offer you a drink?	**Boleh saya ambilkan Anda minuman?** [boleh saja ambilkan anda minuman?]
Would you like to dance?	**Maukah Anda berdansa?** [maukah anda berdansa?]
Let's go to the movies.	**Mari kita ke bioskop.** [mari kita ke bioskop]
May I invite you to ...?	**Boleh saya ajak Anda ke ...?** [boleh saja adʒiaʔ anda ke ...?]
a restaurant	**restoran** [restoran]
the movies	**bioskop** [bioskop]
the theater	**teater** [teater]
go for a walk	**jalan-jalan** [dʒialan-dʒialan]
At what time?	**Jam berapa?** [dʒiam berapa?]
tonight	**malam ini** [malam ini]
at six	**pada pukul enam** [pada pukul enam]
at seven	**pada pukul tujuh** [pada pukul tudʒiuh]
at eight	**pada pukul delapan** [pada pukul delapan]
at nine	**pada pukul sembilan** [pada pukul sembilan]
Do you like it here?	**Apa Anda suka di sini?** [apa anda suka di sini?]
Are you here with someone?	**Apa Anda di sini bersama orang lain?** [apa anda di sini bersama oraŋ lain?]
I'm with my friend.	**Saya bersama teman saya.** [saja bersama teman saja]

I'm with my friends. | **Saya bersama teman-teman saya.**
[saja bersama teman-teman saja]

No, I'm alone. | **Tidak, saya sendirian.**
[tida', saja sendirian]

Do you have a boyfriend? | **Kamu punya pacar?**
[kamu punja patʃar?]

I have a boyfriend. | **Aku punya pacar.**
[aku punja patʃar]

Do you have a girlfriend? | **Kamu punya pacar?**
[kamu punja patʃar?]

I have a girlfriend. | **Aku punya pacar.**
[aku punja patʃar]

Can I see you again? | **Bolehkah aku menemuimu lagi?**
[bolehkah aku menemuimu lagi?]

Can I call you? | **Bolehkah aku meneleponmu?**
[bolehkah aku meneleponmu?]

Call me. (Give me a call.) | **Telepon aku.**
[telepon aku]

What's your number? | **Berapa nomor teleponmu?**
[berapa nomor teleponmu?]

I miss you. | **Aku merindukanmu.**
[aku merindukanmu]

You have a beautiful name. | **Nama Anda bagus.**
[nama anda bagus]

I love you. | **Aku mencintaimu.**
[aku mentʃintajmu]

Will you marry me? | **Maukah kau menikah denganku?**
[maukah kau menikah deŋanku?]

You're kidding! | **Anda bercanda!**
[anda bertʃanda!]

I'm just kidding. | **Saya hanya bercanda.**
[saja hanja bertʃanda]

Are you serious? | **Apa Anda serius?**
[apa anda serius?]

I'm serious. | **Saya serius.**
[saja serius]

Really?! | **Sungguh?!**
[suŋguh?!]

It's unbelievable! | **Tak bisa dipercaya!**
[tak bisa dipertʃaja!]

I don't believe you. | **Saya tidak percaya.**
[saja tida' pertʃaja]

I can't. | **Saya tidak bisa.**
[saja tida' bisa]

I don't know. | **Saya tidak tahu.**
[saja tida' tahu]

I don't understand you. | **Saya tidak mengerti sikap Anda.**
[saja tida' meŋerti sikap anda]

Please go away.

Silakan pergi saja.
[silakan pergi sadʒ'a]

Leave me alone!

Tinggalkan saya sendiri!
[tiŋgalkan saja sendiri!]

I can't stand him.

Saya tidak tahan dengannya.
[saja tida' tahan deŋannja]

You are disgusting!

Anda menjijikkan!
[anda mendʒidʒi'kan!]

I'll call the police!

Saya akan telepon polisi!
[saja akan telepon polisi!]

Sharing impressions. Emotions

I like it.	**Saya menyukainya.** [saja menjukainja]
Very nice.	**Bagus sekali.** [bagus sekali]
That's great!	**Hebat!** [hebat!]
It's not bad.	**Lumayan.** [lumajan]
I don't like it.	**Saya tidak menyukainya.** [saja tidaʔ menjukainja]
It's not good.	**Tidak bagus.** [tidaʔ bagus]
It's bad.	**Jelek.** [dʒ'eleʔ]
It's very bad.	**Jelek sekali.** [dʒ'eleʔ sekali]
It's disgusting.	**Menjijikkan.** [mendʒidʒiʔkan]
I'm happy.	**Saya senang.** [saja senaŋ]
I'm content.	**Saya puas.** [saja puas]
I'm in love.	**Saya sedang jatuh cinta.** [saja sedaŋ dʒ'atuh tʃinta]
I'm calm.	**Saya tenang.** [saja tenaŋ]
I'm bored.	**Saya bosan.** [saja bosan]
I'm tired.	**Saya lelah.** [saja lelah]
I'm sad.	**Saya sedih.** [saja sedih]
I'm frightened.	**Saya takut.** [saja takut]
I'm angry.	**Saya marah.** [saja marah]
I'm worried.	**Saya khawatir.** [saja hawatir]
I'm nervous.	**Saya gugup.** [saja gugup]

I'm jealous. (envious)	**Saya cemburu.**
	[saja tʃemburu]
I'm surprised.	**Saya terkejut.**
	[saja terkeʤut]
I'm perplexed.	**Saya bingung.**
	[saja biŋuŋ]

Problems. Accidents

I've got a problem.	**Saya sedang kesulitan.** [saja sedaŋ kesulitan]
We've got a problem.	**Kami sedang kesulitan.** [kami sedaŋ kesulitan]
I'm lost.	**Saya tersesat.** [saja tersesat]
I missed the last bus (train).	**Saya tertinggal bus (kereta) terakhir.** [saja tertiŋgal bus (kereta) terahir]
I don't have any money left.	**Saya tidak punya uang lagi.** [saja tidak punja uaŋ lagi]

I've lost my …	**… saya hilang.** [… saja hilaŋ]
Someone stole my …	**… saya kecurian.** [… saja ketʃurian]
passport	**paspor** [paspor]
wallet	**dompet** [dompet]
papers	**dokumen** [dokumen]
ticket	**tiket** [tiket]
money	**uang** [uaŋ]
handbag	**tas** [tas]
camera	**kamera** [kamera]
laptop	**laptop** [laptop]
tablet computer	**komputer tablet** [komputer tablet]
mobile phone	**ponsel** [ponsel]

Help me!	**Tolong!** [toloŋ!]
What's happened?	**Ada apa?** [ada apa?]
fire	**kebakaran** [kebakaran]
shooting	**penembakan** [penembakan]

murder	**pembunuhan**
	[pembunuhan]
explosion	**ledakan**
	[ledakan]
fight	**perkelahian**
	[perkelahian]

Call the police!	**Telepon polisi!**
	[telepon polisi!]
Please hurry up!	**Cepat!**
	[tʃepat!]
I'm looking for the police station.	**Saya sedang mencari kantor polisi.**
	[saja sedaŋ mentʃari kantor polisi]
I need to make a call.	**Saya perlu menelepon.**
	[saja perlu menelepon]
May I use your phone?	**Bolehkah saya meminjam telepon Anda?**
	[bolehkah saja memindʒam telepon anda?]

I've been ...	**Saya telah ...**
	[saja telah ...]
mugged	**ditodong**
	[ditodoŋ]
robbed	**dirampok**
	[dirampoʔ]
raped	**diperkosa**
	[diperkosa]
attacked (beaten up)	**diserang**
	[diseraŋ]

Are you all right?	**Anda tidak apa-apa?**
	[anda tidaʔ apa-apa?]
Did you see who it was?	**Apa Anda melihat pelakunya?**
	[apa anda melihat pelakunja?]
Would you be able to recognize the person?	**Bisakah Anda mengenali pelakunya?**
	[bisakah anda meŋenali pelakunja?]
Are you sure?	**Anda yakin?**
	[anda jakin?]

Please calm down.	**Tenanglah dulu.**
	[tenaŋlah dulu]
Take it easy!	**Tenangkan diri Anda!**
	[tenaŋkan diri anda!]
Don't worry!	**Jangan khawatir!**
	[dʒaŋan hawatir!]
Everything will be fine.	**Semuanya akan baik-baik saja.**
	[semuanja akan baiʔ-baiʔ sadʒa]
Everything's all right.	**Semuanya baik-baik saja.**
	[semuanja baiʔ-baiʔ sadʒa]
Come here, please.	**Kemarilah.**
	[kemarilah]

I have some questions for you.

Saya ingin menanyakan beberapa pertanyaan.
[saja iŋin menanjakan beberapa pertanja'an]

Wait a moment, please.

Tunggulah sebentar.
[tuŋgulah sebentar]

Do you have any I.D.?

Apa Anda punya kartu pengenal?
[apa anda punja kartu peŋenal?]

Thanks. You can leave now.

Terima kasih. Anda boleh pergi sekarang.
[terima kasih. anda boleh pergi sekaraŋ]

Hands behind your head!

Tangan di belakang kepala!
[taŋan di belakaŋ kepala!]

You're under arrest!

Anda ditangkap!
[anda ditaŋkap!]

Health problems

Please help me.	**Tolong bantu saya.** [toloŋ bantu saja]
I don't feel well.	**Saya tidak enak badan.** [saja tida' ena' badan]
My husband doesn't feel well.	**Suami saya tidak enak badan.** [suami saja tida' ena' badan]
My son …	**Anak laki-laki saya …** [ana' laki-laki saja …]
My father …	**Ayah saya …** [ajah saja …]
My wife doesn't feel well.	**Istri saya tidak enak badan.** [istri saja tida' ena' badan]
My daughter …	**Anak perempuan saya …** [ana' perempuan saja …]
My mother …	**Ibu saya …** [ibu saja …]
I've got a …	**Saya …** [saja …]
headache	**sakit kepala** [sakit kepala]
sore throat	**sakit tenggorokan** [sakit teŋgorokan]
stomach ache	**sakit perut** [sakit perut]
toothache	**sakit gigi** [sakit gigi]
I feel dizzy.	**Saya merasa pusing.** [saja merasa pusiŋ]
He has a fever.	**Dia demam.** [dia demam]
She has a fever.	**Dia demam.** [dia demam]
I can't breathe.	**Saya tak dapat bernapas.** [saja ta' dapat bernapas]
I'm short of breath.	**Saya sesak napas.** [saja sesa' napas]
I am asthmatic.	**Saya menderita asma.** [saja menderita asma]
I am diabetic.	**Saya menderita diabetes.** [saja menderita diabetes]

| I can't sleep. | **Saya susah tidur.**
[saja susah tidur] |
| food poisoning | **keracunan makanan**
[keratʃunan makanan] |

It hurts here.	**Sakitnya di sini.** [sakitnʲa di sini]
Help me!	**Tolong!** [tolonʲ!]
I am here!	**Saya di sini!** [saja di sini!]
We are here!	**Kami di sini!** [kami di sini!]
Get me out of here!	**Keluarkan saya dari sini!** [keluarkan saja dari sini!]
I need a doctor.	**Saya perlu dokter.** [saja perlu dokter]
I can't move.	**Saya tak dapat bergerak.** [saja taʼ dapat bergeraʼ]
I can't move my legs.	**Kaki saya tak dapat digerakkan.** [kaki saja taʼ dapat digeraʼkan]

I have a wound.	**Saya terluka.** [saja terluka]
Is it serious?	**Apakah serius?** [apakah serius?]
My documents are in my pocket.	**Dokumen saya ada di saku.** [dokumen saja ada di saku]
Calm down!	**Tenanglah dulu!** [tenaŋlah dulu!]
May I use your phone?	**Bolehkah saya meminjam telepon Anda?** [bolehkah saja memindʒʲam telepon anda?]

Call an ambulance!	**Panggil ambulans!** [paŋgil ambulans!]
It's urgent!	**Ini mendesak!** [ini mendesaʼ!]
It's an emergency!	**Ini darurat!** [ini darurat!]
Please hurry up!	**Cepat!** [tʃepat!]
Would you please call a doctor?	**Maukah Anda memanggilkan dokter?** [maukah anda memaŋgilkan dokter?]
Where is the hospital?	**Di mana rumah sakitnya?** [di mana rumah sakitnʲa?]

| How are you feeling? | **Bagaimana perasaan Anda?**
[bagajmana perasaʼan anda?] |
| Are you all right? | **Anda tidak apa-apa?**
[anda tidaʼ apa-apa?] |

What's happened?	**Ada apa?** [ada apa?]
I feel better now.	**Saya merasa baikan sekarang.** [saja merasa baikan sekaraŋ]
It's OK.	**Tidak apa-apa.** [tida' apa-apa]
It's all right.	**Tidak apa-apa.** [tida' apa-apa]

At the pharmacy

pharmacy (drugstore)	**apotek** [apote']
24-hour pharmacy	**apotek 24 jam** [apote' dua puluh empat dʒ̣am]
Where is the closest pharmacy?	**Di mana apotek terdekat?** [di mana apote' terdekat?]
Is it open now?	**Apa buka sekarang?** [apa buka sekaraŋ?]
At what time does it open?	**Pukup berapa buka?** [pukup berapa buka?]
At what time does it close?	**Pukul berapa tutup?** [pukul berapa tutup?]
Is it far?	**Apakah tempatnya jauh?** [apakah tempatnja dʒ̣auh?]
Can I get there on foot?	**Bisakah saya berjalan kaki ke sana?** [bisakah saja berdʒ̣alan kaki ke sana?]
Can you show me on the map?	**Bisakah Anda tunjukkan di peta?** [bisakah anda tundʒ̣u'kan di peta?]
Please give me something for ...	**Berikan saya obat untuk ...** [berikan saja obat untu' ...]
a headache	**sakit kepala** [sakit kepala]
a cough	**batuk** [batu']
a cold	**masuk angin** [masu' aŋin]
the flu	**flu** [flu]
a fever	**demam** [demam]
a stomach ache	**sakit perut** [sakit perut]
nausea	**mual** [mual]
diarrhea	**diare** [diare]
constipation	**sembelit** [sembelit]
pain in the back	**nyeri punggung** [njeri puŋguŋ]

chest pain	**nyeri dada** [njeri dada]
side stitch	**kram perut** [kram perut]
abdominal pain	**nyeri perut** [njeri perut]
pill	**pil** [pil]
ointment, cream	**salep, krim** [salep, krim]
syrup	**sirop** [sirop]
spray	**semprot** [semprot]
drops	**tetes** [tetes]
You need to go to the hospital.	**Anda perlu ke rumah sakit.** [anda perlu ke rumah sakit]
health insurance	**asuransi kesehatan** [asuransi kesehatan]
prescription	**resep** [resep]
insect repellant	**obat antinyamuk** [obat antinjamu?]
Band Aid	**plester pembalut** [plester pembalut]

The bare minimum

Excuse me, ...	**Permisi, ...** [permisi, ...]
Hello.	**Halo.** [halo]
Thank you.	**Terima kasih.** [terima kasih]
Good bye.	**Selamat tinggal.** [slamat tiŋgal]
Yes.	**Ya.** [ja]
No.	**Tidak.** [tida']
I don't know.	**Saya tidak tahu.** [saja tida' tahu]
Where?	Where to?	When?	**Di mana?	Ke mana?	Kapan?** [di mana?	ke mana?	kapan?]
I need ...	**Saya perlu ...** [saja perlu ...]
I want ...	**Saya ingin ...** [saja iŋin ...]
Do you have ...?	**Apa Anda punya ...?** [apa anda punja ...?]
Is there a ... here?	**Apa ada ... di sini?** [apa ada ... di sini?]
May I ...?	**Boleh saya ...?** [boleh saja ...?]
..., please (polite request)	**Tolong, ...** [toloŋ, ...]
I'm looking for ...	**Saya sedang mencari ...** [saja sedaŋ mentʃari ...]
restroom	**kamar kecil** [kamar ketʃil]
ATM	**ATM** [a-te-em]
pharmacy (drugstore)	**apotek** [apote']
hospital	**rumah sakit** [rumah sakit]
police station	**kantor polisi** [kantor polisi]
subway	**stasiun bawah tanah** [stasiun bawah tanah]

taxi	**taksi** [taksi]
train station	**stasiun kereta api** [stasiun kereta api]

My name is …	**Nama saya …** [nama saja …]
What's your name?	**Siapa nama Anda?** [siapa nama anda?]
Could you please help me?	**Bisakah Anda menolong saya?** [bisakah anda menoloŋ saja?]
I've got a problem.	**Saya sedang kesulitan.** [saja sedaŋ kesulitan]
I don't feel well.	**Saya tidak enak badan.** [saja tida' enak badan]
Call an ambulance!	**Panggil ambulans!** [paŋgil ambulans!]
May I make a call?	**Boleh saya menelepon?** [boleh saja menelepon?]

I'm sorry.	**Maaf.** [ma'af]
You're welcome.	**Terima kasih kembali.** [terima kasih kembali]

I, me	**Saya, aku** [saja, aku]
you (inform.)	**kamu, kau** [kamu, kau]
he	**dia, ia** [dia, ia]
she	**dia, ia** [dia, ia]
they (masc.)	**mereka** [mereka]
they (fem.)	**mereka** [mereka]
we	**kami** [kami]
you (pl)	**kalian** [kalian]
you (sg, form.)	**Anda** [anda]

ENTRANCE	**MASUK** [masu']
EXIT	**KELUAR** [keluar]
OUT OF ORDER	**TIDAK DAPAT DIGUNAKAN** [tida' dapat digunakan]
CLOSED	**TUTUP** [tutup]

OPEN

BUKA
[buka]

FOR WOMEN

UNTUK PEREMPUAN
[untu' perempuan]

FOR MEN

UNTUK LAKI-LAKI
[untu' laki-laki]

CONCISE
DICTIONARY

This section contains more
than 1,500 useful words
arranged alphabetically.
The dictionary includes a lot
of gastronomic terms and
will be helpful when ordering
food at a restaurant or buying
groceries

T&P Books Publishing

DICTIONARY CONTENTS

T&P Books Publishing

time	**waktu**	[waktu]
hour	**jam**	[dʒʲam]
half an hour	**setengah jam**	[seteŋah dʒʲam]
minute	**menit**	[menit]
second	**detik**	[detiʔ]

today (adv)	**hari ini**	[hari ini]
tomorrow (adv)	**besok**	[besoʔ]
yesterday (adv)	**kemarin**	[kemarin]

Monday	**Hari Senin**	[hari senin]
Tuesday	**Hari Selasa**	[hari selasa]
Wednesday	**Hari Rabu**	[hari rabu]
Thursday	**Hari Kamis**	[hari kamis]
Friday	**Hari Jumat**	[hari dʒʲumat]
Saturday	**Hari Sabtu**	[hari sabtu]
Sunday	**Hari Minggu**	[hari miŋgu]

day	**hari**	[hari]
working day	**hari kerja**	[hari kerdʒʲa]
public holiday	**hari libur**	[hari libur]
weekend	**akhir pekan**	[ahir pekan]

week	**minggu**	[miŋgu]
last week (adv)	**minggu lalu**	[miŋgu lalu]
next week (adv)	**minggu berikutnya**	[miŋgu bərikutnja]

| sunrise | **matahari terbit** | [matahari tərbit] |
| sunset | **matahari terbenam** | [matahari tərbenam] |

| in the morning | **pada pagi hari** | [pada pagi hari] |
| in the afternoon | **pada sore hari** | [pada sore hari] |

| in the evening | **waktu sore** | [waktu sore] |
| tonight (this evening) | **sore ini** | [sore ini] |

| at night | **pada malam hari** | [pada malam hari] |
| midnight | **tengah malam** | [teŋah malam] |

January	**Januari**	[dʒʲanuari]
February	**Februari**	[februari]
March	**Maret**	[maret]
April	**April**	[april]
May	**Mei**	[mei]
June	**Juni**	[dʒʲuni]

July	**Juli**	[dʒˈuli]
August	**Augustus**	[augustus]
September	**September**	[september]
October	**Oktober**	[oktober]
November	**November**	[november]
December	**Desember**	[desember]
in spring	**pada musim semi**	[pada musim semi]
in summer	**pada musim panas**	[pada musim panas]
in fall	**pada musim gugur**	[pada musim gugur]
in winter	**pada musim dingin**	[pada musim diŋin]
month	**bulan**	[bulan]
season (summer, etc.)	**musim**	[musim]
year	**tahun**	[tahun]
century	**abad**	[abad]

2. Numbers. Numerals

digit, figure	**angka**	[aŋka]
number	**nomor**	[nomor]
minus sign	**minus**	[minus]
plus sign	**plus**	[plus]
sum, total	**jumlah**	[dʒˈumlah]
first (adj)	**pertama**	[pərtama]
second (adj)	**kedua**	[kedua]
third (adj)	**ketiga**	[ketiga]
0 zero	**nol**	[nol]
1 one	**satu**	[satu]
2 two	**dua**	[dua]
3 three	**tiga**	[tiga]
4 four	**empat**	[empat]
5 five	**lima**	[lima]
6 six	**enam**	[enam]
7 seven	**tujuh**	[tudʒˈuh]
8 eight	**delapan**	[delapan]
9 nine	**sembilan**	[sembilan]
10 ten	**sepuluh**	[sepuluh]
11 eleven	**sebelas**	[sebelas]
12 twelve	**dua belas**	[dua belas]
13 thirteen	**tiga belas**	[tiga belas]
14 fourteen	**empat belas**	[empat belas]
15 fifteen	**lima belas**	[lima belas]
16 sixteen	**enam belas**	[enam belas]
17 seventeen	**tujuh belas**	[tudʒˈuh belas]

18 eighteen	delapan belas	[delapan belas]
19 nineteen	sembilan belas	[sembilan belas]
20 twenty	dua puluh	[dua puluh]
30 thirty	tiga puluh	[tiga puluh]
40 forty	empat puluh	[empat puluh]
50 fifty	lima puluh	[lima puluh]
60 sixty	enam puluh	[enam puluh]
70 seventy	tujuh puluh	[tuʤʲuh puluh]
80 eighty	delapan puluh	[delapan puluh]
90 ninety	sembilan puluh	[sembilan puluh]
100 one hundred	seratus	[seratus]
200 two hundred	dua ratus	[dua ratus]
300 three hundred	tiga ratus	[tiga ratus]
400 four hundred	empat ratus	[empat ratus]
500 five hundred	lima ratus	[lima ratus]
600 six hundred	enam ratus	[enam ratus]
700 seven hundred	tujuh ratus	[tuʤʲuh ratus]
800 eight hundred	delapan ratus	[delapan ratus]
900 nine hundred	sembilan ratus	[sembilan ratus]
1000 one thousand	seribu	[seribu]
10000 ten thousand	sepuluh ribu	[sepuluh ribu]
one hundred thousand	seratus ribu	[seratus ribu]
million	juta	[ʤʲuta]
billion	miliar	[miliar]

3. Humans. Family

man (adult male)	laki-laki, pria	[laki-laki], [pria]
young man	pemuda	[pemuda]
teenager	remaja	[remaʤʲa]
woman	perempuan, wanita	[perempuan], [wanita]
girl (young woman)	gadis	[gadis]
age	umur	[umur]
adult (adj)	dewasa	[dewasa]
middle-aged (adj)	paruh baya	[paruh baja]
elderly (adj)	lansia	[lansia]
old (adj)	tua	[tua]
old man	lelaki tua	[lelaki tua]
old woman	perempuan tua	[perempuan tua]
retirement	pensiun	[pensiun]
to retire (from job)	pensiun	[pensiun]
retiree	pensiunan	[pensiunan]

mother	ibu	[ibu]
father	ayah	[ajah]
son	anak lelaki	[anaʔ lelaki]
daughter	anak perempuan	[anaʔ pərempuan]
brother	saudara lelaki	[saudara lelaki]
elder brother	kakak lelaki	[kakaʔ lelaki]
younger brother	adik lelaki	[adiʔ lelaki]
sister	saudara perempuan	[saudara pərempuan]
elder sister	kakak perempuan	[kakaʔ pərempuan]
younger sister	adik perempuan	[adiʔ pərempuan]
parents	orang tua	[oraŋ tua]
child	anak	[anaʔ]
children	anak-anak	[anaʔ-anaʔ]
stepmother	ibu tiri	[ibu tiri]
stepfather	ayah tiri	[ajah tiri]
grandmother	nenek	[neneʔ]
grandfather	kakek	[kakeʔ]
grandson	cucu laki-laki	[ʧuʧu laki-laki]
granddaughter	cucu perempuan	[ʧuʧu pərempuan]
grandchildren	cucu	[ʧuʧu]
uncle	paman	[paman]
aunt	bibi	[bibi]
nephew	keponakan laki-laki	[keponakan laki-laki]
niece	keponakan perempuan	[keponakan pərempuan]
wife	istri	[istri]
husband	suami	[suami]
married (masc.)	menikah, beristri	[mənikah], [bəristri]
married (fem.)	menikah, bersuami	[mənikah], [bərsuami]
widow	janda	[dʒʲanda]
widower	duda	[duda]
name (first name)	nama, nama depan	[nama], [nama depan]
surname (last name)	nama keluarga	[nama keluarga]
relative	kerabat	[kerabat]
friend (masc.)	sahabat	[sahabat]
friendship	persahabatan	[pərsahabatan]
partner	mitra	[mitra]
superior (n)	atasan	[atasan]
colleague	kolega	[kolega]
neighbors	para tetangga	[para tetaŋga]

4. Human body

| organism (body) | organisme | [organisme] |
| body | tubuh | [tubuh] |

heart	jantung	[ʤantuŋ]
blood	darah	[darah]
brain	otak	[otaʔ]
nerve	saraf	[saraf]

bone	tulang	[tulaŋ]
skeleton	skelet, rangka	[skelet], [raŋka]
spine (backbone)	tulang belakang	[tulaŋ belakaŋ]
rib	tulang rusuk	[tulaŋ rusuʔ]
skull	tengkorak	[teŋkoraʔ]

muscle	otot	[otot]
lungs	paru-paru	[paru-paru]
skin	kulit	[kulit]

head	kepala	[kepala]
face	wajah	[waʤah]
nose	hidung	[hiduŋ]
forehead	dahi	[dahi]
cheek	pipi	[pipi]

mouth	mulut	[mulut]
tongue	lidah	[lidah]
tooth	gigi	[gigi]
lips	bibir	[bibir]
chin	dagu	[dagu]

ear	telinga	[teliŋa]
neck	leher	[leher]
throat	tenggorok	[teŋgoroʔ]

eye	mata	[mata]
pupil	pupil, biji mata	[pupil], [biʤi mata]
eyebrow	alis	[alis]
eyelash	bulu mata	[bulu mata]

hair	rambut	[rambut]
hairstyle	tatanan rambut	[tatanan rambut]
mustache	kumis	[kumis]
beard	janggut	[ʤaŋgut]
to have (a beard, etc.)	memelihara	[memelihara]
bald (adj)	botak, plontos	[botak], [plontos]

hand	tangan	[taŋan]
arm	lengan	[leŋan]
finger	jari	[ʤari]
nail	kuku	[kuku]
palm	telapak	[telapaʔ]

shoulder	bahu	[bahu]
leg	kaki	[kaki]
foot	telapak kaki	[telapaʔ kaki]

knee	lutut	[lutut]
heel	tumit	[tumit]

back	punggung	[puŋguŋ]
waist	pinggang	[piŋgaŋ]
beauty mark	tanda lahir	[tanda lahir]
birthmark	tanda lahir	[tanda lahir]
(café au lait spot)		

5. Medicine. Diseases. Drugs

health	kesehatan	[kesehatan]
well (not sick)	sehat	[sehat]
sickness	penyakit	[penjakit]
to be sick	sakit	[sakit]
ill, sick (adj)	sakit	[sakit]

cold (illness)	pilek, selesma	[pilek], [selesma]
to catch a cold	masuk angin	[masu' aɲin]
tonsillitis	radang tonsil	[radaŋ tonsil]
pneumonia	radang paru-paru	[radaŋ paru-paru]
flu, influenza	flu	[flu]

runny nose (coryza)	hidung meler	[hiduŋ meler]
cough	batuk	[batu']
to cough (vi)	batuk	[batu']
to sneeze (vi)	bersin	[bersin]

stroke	stroke	[stroke]
heart attack	infark	[infar']
allergy	alergi	[alergi]
asthma	asma	[asma]
diabetes	diabetes	[diabetes]

tumor	tumor	[tumor]
cancer	kanker	[kanker]
alcoholism	alkoholisme	[alkoholisme]
AIDS	AIDS	[ajds]
fever	demam	[demam]
seasickness	mabuk laut	[mabu' laut]

bruise (hématome)	luka memar	[luka memar]
bump (lump)	bengkak	[beŋka']
to limp (vi)	pincang	[pintʃaŋ]
dislocation	keseleo	[keseleo]
to dislocate (vt)	keseleo	[keseleo]

fracture	fraktura, patah tulang	[fraktura], [patah tulaŋ]
burn (injury)	luka bakar	[luka bakar]
injury	cedera	[tʃedera]

pain, ache	**sakit**	[sakit]
toothache	**sakit gigi**	[sakit gigi]
to sweat (perspire)	**berkeringat**	[bərkeriŋat]
deaf (adj)	**tunarungu**	[tunaruŋu]
mute (adj)	**tunawicara**	[tunawitʃara]
immunity	**imunitas**	[imunitas]
virus	**virus**	[virus]
microbe	**mikroba**	[mikroba]
bacterium	**bakteri**	[bakteri]
infection	**infeksi**	[infeksi]
hospital	**rumah sakit**	[rumah sakit]
cure	**perawatan**	[pərawatan]
to vaccinate (vt)	**memvaksinasi**	[memvaksinasi]
to be in a coma	**dalam keadaan koma**	[dalam keada'an koma]
intensive care	**perawatan intensif**	[pərawatan intensif]
symptom	**gejala**	[gedʒ'ala]
pulse	**denyut nadi**	[denyut nadi]

6. Feelings. Emotions. Conversation

I, me	**saya, aku**	[saja], [aku]
you	**engkau, kamu**	[eŋkau], [kamu]
he, she, it	**beliau, dia, ia**	[beliau], [dia], [ia]
we	**kami, kita**	[kami], [kita]
you (to a group)	**kalian**	[kalian]
you (polite, sing.)	**Anda**	[anda]
you (polite, pl)	**Anda sekalian**	[anda sekalian]
they	**mereka**	[mereka]
Hello! (fam.)	**Halo!**	[halo!]
Hello! (form.)	**Halo!**	[halo!]
Good morning!	**Selamat pagi!**	[slamat pagi!]
Good afternoon!	**Selamat siang!**	[slamat siaŋ!]
Good evening!	**Selamat sore!**	[slamat sore!]
to say hello	**menyapa**	[mənjapa]
to greet (vt)	**menyambut**	[mənjambut]
How are you?	**Apa kabar?**	[apa kabar?]
Goodbye! (form.)	**Selamat tinggal!**	[slamat tiŋgal!],
	Selamat jalan!	[slamat dʒ'alan!]
Bye! (fam.)	**Dadah!**	[dadah!]
Thank you!	**Terima kasih!**	[tərima kasih!]
feelings	**perasaan**	[pərasa'an]
to be hungry	**lapar**	[lapar]
to be thirsty	**haus**	[haus]
tired (adj)	**lelah**	[lelah]

to be worried	**khawatir**	[hawatir]
to be nervous	**gugup, gelisah**	[gugup], [gelisah]
hope	**harapan**	[harapan]
to hope (vi, vt)	**berharap**	[bərharap]
character	**watak**	[wata']
modest (adj)	**rendah hati**	[rendah hati]
lazy (adj)	**malas**	[malas]
generous (adj)	**murah hati**	[murah hati]
talented (adj)	**berbakat**	[bərbakat]
honest (adj)	**jujur**	[dʒʲudʒʲur]
serious (adj)	**serius**	[serius]
shy, timid (adj)	**malu**	[malu]
sincere (adj)	**ikhlas**	[ihlas]
coward	**penakut**	[penakut]
to sleep (vi)	**tidur**	[tidur]
dream	**mimpi**	[mimpi]
bed	**ranjang**	[randʒʲaŋ]
pillow	**bantal**	[bantal]
insomnia	**insomnia**	[insomnia]
to go to bed	**tidur**	[tidur]
nightmare	**mimpi buruk**	[mimpi buru']
alarm clock	**weker**	[weker]
smile	**senyuman**	[senyuman]
to smile (vi)	**tersenyum**	[tərsenyum]
to laugh (vi)	**tertawa**	[tərtawa]
quarrel	**pertengkaran**	[pərteŋkaran]
insult	**penghinaan**	[peŋhina'an]
resentment	**perasaan tersinggung**	[pərasa'an tərsiŋguŋ]
angry (mad)	**marah**	[marah]

7. Clothing. Personal accessories

clothes	**pakaian**	[pakajan]
coat (overcoat)	**mantel**	[mantel]
fur coat	**mantel bulu**	[mantel bulu]
jacket (e.g., leather ~)	**jaket**	[dʒʲaket]
raincoat (trenchcoat, etc.)	**jas hujan**	[dʒʲas hudʒʲan]
shirt (button shirt)	**kemeja**	[kemedʒʲa]
pants	**celana**	[tʃelana]
suit jacket	**jas**	[dʒʲas]
suit	**setelan**	[setelan]
dress (frock)	**gaun**	[gaun]
skirt	**rok**	[ro']

T-shirt	baju kaus	[baʤʲu kaus]
bathrobe	jubah mandi	[ʤʲubah mandi]
pajamas	piyama	[piyama]
workwear	pakaian kerja	[pakajan kerʤʲa]

underwear	pakaian dalam	[pakajan dalam]
socks	kaus kaki	[kaus kaki]
bra	beha	[beha]
pantyhose	pantihos	[pantihos]
stockings (thigh highs)	kaus kaki panjang	[kaus kaki panʤʲaŋ]
bathing suit	baju renang	[baʤʲu renaŋ]

hat	topi	[topi]
footwear	sepatu	[sepatu]
boots (e.g., cowboy ~)	sepatu lars	[sepatu lars]
heel	tumit	[tumit]
shoestring	tali sepatu	[tali sepatu]
shoe polish	semir sepatu	[semir sepatu]
cotton (n)	katun	[katun]
wool (n)	wol	[wol]
fur (n)	kulit berbulu	[kulit bərbulu]

gloves	sarung tangan	[saruŋ taŋan]
mittens	sarung tangan	[saruŋ taŋan]
scarf (muffler)	selendang	[selendaŋ]
glasses (eyeglasses)	kacamata	[katʃamata]
umbrella	payung	[pajuŋ]

tie (necktie)	dasi	[dasi]
handkerchief	sapu tangan	[sapu taŋan]
comb	sisir	[sisir]
hairbrush	sikat rambut	[sikat rambut]
buckle	gesper	[gesper]
belt	sabuk	[sabuʔ]
purse	tas tangan	[tas taŋan]

collar	kerah	[kerah]
pocket	saku	[saku]
sleeve	lengan	[leŋan]
fly (on trousers)	golbi	[golbi]

zipper (fastener)	ritsleting	[ritsletiŋ]
button	kancing	[kantʃĩŋ]
to get dirty (vi)	kena kotor	[kena kotor]
stain (mark, spot)	bercak	[bertʃaʔ]

8. City. Urban institutions

| store | toko | [toko] |
| shopping mall | toserba | [toserba] |

supermarket	**pasar swalayan**	[pasar swalajan]
shoe store	**toko sepatu**	[toko sepatu]
bookstore	**toko buku**	[toko buku]
drugstore, pharmacy	**apotek, toko obat**	[apotek], [toko obat]
bakery	**toko roti**	[toko roti]
pastry shop	**toko kue**	[toko kue]
grocery store	**toko pangan**	[toko paŋan]
butcher shop	**toko daging**	[toko dagiŋ]
produce store	**toko sayur**	[toko sajur]
market	**pasar**	[pasar]
hair salon	**salon rambut**	[salon rambut]
post office	**kantor pos**	[kantor pos]
dry cleaners	**penatu kimia**	[penatu kimia]
circus	**sirkus**	[sirkus]
zoo	**kebun binatang**	[kebun binataŋ]
theater	**teater**	[teater]
movie theater	**bioskop**	[bioskop]
museum	**museum**	[museum]
library	**perpustakaan**	[pərpustakaʔan]
mosque	**masjid**	[masdʒid]
synagogue	**sinagoga, kanisah**	[sinagoga], [kanisah]
cathedral	**katedral**	[katedral]
temple	**kuil, candi**	[kuil], [tʃandi]
church	**gereja**	[geredʒʲa]
college	**institut, perguruan tinggi**	[institut], [pərguruan tiŋgi]
university	**universitas**	[universitas]
school	**sekolah**	[sekolah]
hotel	**hotel**	[hotel]
bank	**bank**	[banʔ]
embassy	**kedutaan besar**	[kedutaʔan besar]
travel agency	**kantor pariwisata**	[kantor pariwisata]
subway	**kereta api bawah tanah**	[kereta api bawah tanah]
hospital	**rumah sakit**	[rumah sakit]
gas station	**SPBU, stasiun bensin**	[es-pe-be-u], [stasjun bensin]
parking lot	**tempat parkir**	[tempat parkir]
ENTRANCE	**MASUK**	[masuʔ]
EXIT	**KELUAR**	[keluar]
PUSH	**DORONG**	[doroŋ]
PULL	**TARIK**	[tariʔ]
OPEN	**BUKA**	[buka]
CLOSED	**TUTUP**	[tutup]
monument	**monumen, patung**	[monumen], [patuŋ]
fortress	**benteng**	[benteŋ]

palace	istana	[istana]
medieval (adj)	abad pertengahan	[abad pərteŋahan]
ancient (adj)	kuno	[kuno]
national (adj)	nasional	[nasional]
famous (monument, etc.)	terkenal	[tərkenal]

9. Money. Finances

money	uang	[uaŋ]
coin	koin	[koin]
dollar	dolar	[dolar]
euro	euro	[euro]

ATM	Anjungan Tunai Mandiri, ATM	[andʒuŋan tunaj mandiri], [a-te-em]
currency exchange	kantor penukaran uang	[kantor penukaran uaŋ]
exchange rate	nilai tukar	[nilaj tukar]
cash	uang kontan, uang tunai	[uaŋ kontan], [uaŋ tunaj]

How much?	Berapa?	[bərapa?]
to pay (vi, vt)	membayar	[membajar]
payment	pembayaran	[pembajaran]
change (give the ~)	kembalian	[kembalian]

price	harga	[harga]
discount	diskon	[diskon]
cheap (adj)	murah	[murah]
expensive (adj)	mahal	[mahal]

bank	bank	[banʔ]
account	rekening	[rekeniŋ]
credit card	kartu kredit	[kartu kredit]
check	cek	[tʃeʔ]
to write a check	menulis cek	[mənulis tʃeʔ]
checkbook	buku cek	[buku tʃeʔ]

debt	utang	[utaŋ]
debtor	pengutang	[peŋutaŋ]
to lend (money)	meminjamkan	[memindʒʲamkan]
to borrow (vi, vt)	meminjam	[memindʒʲam]

to rent (~ a tuxedo)	menyewa	[mənjewa]
on credit (adv)	secara kredit	[setʃara kredit]
wallet	dompet	[dompet]
safe	brankas	[brankas]
inheritance	warisan	[warisan]
fortune (wealth)	kekayaan	[kekaja'an]

| tax | pajak | [padʒʲaʔ] |
| fine | denda | [denda] |

to fine (vt)	mendenda	[məndenda]
wholesale (adj)	grosir	[grosir]
retail (adj)	eceran	[etʃeran]
to insure (vt)	mengasuransikan	[məŋasuransikan]
insurance	asuransi	[asuransi]

capital	modal	[modal]
turnover	omzet	[omzet]
stock (share)	saham	[saham]
profit	profit, untung	[profit], [untuŋ]
profitable (adj)	beruntung	[bəruntuŋ]

crisis	krisis	[krisis]
bankruptcy	kebangkrutan	[kebaŋkrutan]
to go bankrupt	jatuh bangkrut	[dʒʲatuh baŋkrut]

accountant	akuntan	[akuntan]
salary	gaji, upah	[gadʒi], [upah]
bonus (money)	bonus	[bonus]

10. Transportation

bus	bus	[bus]
streetcar	trem	[trem]
trolley bus	bus listrik	[bus listriʔ]

to go by ...	naik ...	[naiʔ ...]
to get on (~ the bus)	naik	[naiʔ]
to get off ...	turun ...	[turun ...]

stop (e.g., bus ~)	halte, pemberhentian	[halte], [pemberhentian]
terminus	halte terakhir	[halte tərahir]
schedule	jadwal	[dʒʲadwal]
ticket	tiket	[tiket]
to be late (for ...)	terlambat ...	[tərlambat ...]

taxi, cab	taksi	[taksi]
by taxi	naik taksi	[naiʔ taksi]
taxi stand	pangkalan taksi	[paŋkalan taksi]

traffic	lalu lintas	[lalu lintas]
rush hour	jam sibuk	[dʒʲam sibuʔ]
to park (vi)	parkir	[parkir]

subway	kereta api bawah tanah	[kereta api bawah tanah]
station	stasiun	[stasiun]
train	kereta api	[kereta api]
train station	stasiun kereta api	[stasiun kereta api]
rails	rel	[rel]
compartment	kabin	[kabin]

berth	**bangku**	[baŋku]
airplane	**pesawat terbang**	[pesawat tərbaŋ]
air ticket	**tiket pesawat terbang**	[tiket pesawat tərbaŋ]
airline	**maskapai penerbangan**	[maskapaj penerbaŋan]
airport	**bandara**	[bandara]
flight (act of flying)	**penerbangan**	[penerbaŋan]
luggage	**bagasi**	[bagasi]
luggage cart	**troli bagasi**	[troli bagasi]
ship	**kapal**	[kapal]
cruise ship	**kapal laut**	[kapal laut]
yacht	**perahu pesiar**	[pərahu pesiar]
boat (flat-bottomed ~)	**perahu**	[pərahu]
captain	**kapten**	[kapten]
cabin	**kabin**	[kabin]
port (harbor)	**pelabuhan**	[pelabuhan]
bicycle	**sepeda**	[sepeda]
scooter	**skuter**	[skuter]
motorcycle, bike	**sepeda motor**	[sepeda motor]
pedal	**pedal**	[pedal]
pump	**pompa**	[pompa]
wheel	**roda**	[roda]
automobile, car	**mobil**	[mobil]
ambulance	**ambulans**	[ambulans]
truck	**truk**	[truʔ]
used (adj)	**bekas**	[bekas]
car crash	**kecelakaan mobil**	[ketʃelakaʔan mobil]
repair	**reparasi**	[reparasi]

11. Food. Part 1

meat	**daging**	[dagiŋ]
chicken	**ayam**	[ajam]
duck	**bebek**	[bebeʔ]
pork	**daging babi**	[dagiŋ babi]
veal	**daging anak sapi**	[dagiŋ anaʔ sapi]
lamb	**daging domba**	[dagiŋ domba]
beef	**daging sapi**	[dagiŋ sapi]
sausage (bologna, pepperoni, etc.)	**sosis**	[sosis]
egg	**telur**	[telur]
fish	**ikan**	[ikan]
cheese	**keju**	[kedʒʲu]
sugar	**gula**	[gula]

salt	**garam**	[garam]
rice	**beras, nasi**	[beras], [nasi]
pasta (macaroni)	**makaroni**	[makaroni]
butter	**mentega**	[məntega]
vegetable oil	**minyak nabati**	[minja' nabati]
bread	**roti**	[roti]
chocolate (n)	**cokelat**	[tʃokelat]
wine	**anggur**	[aŋgur]
coffee	**kopi**	[kopi]
milk	**susu**	[susu]
juice	**jus**	[dʒʲus]
beer	**bir**	[bir]
tea	**teh**	[teh]
tomato	**tomat**	[tomat]
cucumber	**mentimun, ketimun**	[məntimun], [ketimun]
carrot	**wortel**	[wortel]
potato	**kentang**	[kentaŋ]
onion	**bawang**	[bawaŋ]
garlic	**bawang putih**	[bawaŋ putih]
cabbage	**kol**	[kol]
beetroot	**ubi bit merah**	[ubi bit merah]
eggplant	**terung, terong**	[teruŋ], [təroŋ]
dill	**adas sowa**	[adas sowa]
lettuce	**selada**	[selada]
corn (maize)	**jagung**	[dʒʲaguŋ]
fruit	**buah**	[buah]
apple	**apel**	[apel]
pear	**pir**	[pir]
lemon	**jeruk sitrun**	[dʒʲeru' sitrun]
orange	**jeruk manis**	[dʒʲeru' manis]
strawberry (garden ~)	**stroberi**	[stroberi]
plum	**plum**	[plum]
raspberry	**buah frambus**	[buah frambus]
pineapple	**nanas**	[nanas]
banana	**pisang**	[pisaŋ]
watermelon	**semangka**	[semaŋka]
grape	**buah anggur**	[buah aŋgur]
melon	**melon**	[melon]

12. Food. Part 2

cuisine	**masakan**	[masakan]
recipe	**resep**	[resep]
food	**makanan**	[makanan]
to have breakfast	**sarapan**	[sarapan]

| to have lunch | makan siang | [makan siaŋ] |
| to have dinner | makan malam | [makan malam] |

taste, flavor	rasa	[rasa]
tasty (adj)	enak	[ena']
cold (adj)	dingin	[diŋin]
hot (adj)	panas	[panas]
sweet (sugary)	manis	[manis]
salty (adj)	asin	[asin]

sandwich (bread)	roti lapis	[roti lapis]
side dish	lauk	[lau']
filling (for cake, pie)	inti	[inti]
sauce	saus	[saus]
piece (of cake, pie)	potongan	[potoŋan]

diet	diet, pola makan	[diet], [pola makan]
vitamin	vitamin	[vitamin]
calorie	kalori	[kalori]
vegetarian (n)	vegetarian	[vegetarian]

restaurant	restoran	[restoran]
coffee house	warung kopi	[waruŋ kopi]
appetite	nafsu makan	[nafsu makan]
Enjoy your meal!	Selamat makan!	[selamat makan!]

waiter	pelayan lelaki	[pelajan lelaki]
waitress	pelayan perempuan	[pelajan pərempuan]
bartender	pelayan bar	[pelajan bar]
menu	menu	[menu]

spoon	sendok	[sendo']
knife	pisau	[pisau]
fork	garpu	[garpu]
cup (e.g., coffee ~)	cangkir	[ʧaŋkir]

plate (dinner ~)	piring	[piriŋ]
saucer	alas cangkir	[alas ʧaŋkir]
napkin (on table)	serbet	[serbet]
toothpick	tusuk gigi	[tusu' gigi]

to order (meal)	memesan	[memesan]
course, dish	masakan, hidangan	[masakan], [hidaŋan]
portion	porsi	[porsi]
appetizer	makanan ringan	[makanan riŋan]
salad	salada	[salada]
soup	sup	[sup]

dessert	hidangan penutup	[hidaŋan penutup]
jam (whole fruit jam)	selai buah utuh	[selaj buah utuh]
ice-cream	es krim	[es krim]
check	bon	[bon]

| to pay the check | membayar bon | [membajar bon] |
| tip | tip | [tip] |

13. House. Apartment. Part 1

house	rumah	[rumah]
country house	rumah luar kota	[rumah luar kota]
villa (seaside ~)	vila	[vila]

floor, story	lantai	[lantaj]
entrance	pintu masuk	[pintu masuʔ]
wall	dinding	[dindiŋ]
roof	atap	[atap]
chimney	cerobong	[tʃeroboŋ]
attic (storage place)	loteng	[loteŋ]
window	jendela	[dʒiendela]
window ledge	ambang jendela	[ambaŋ dʒiendela]
balcony	balkon	[balkon]

stairs (stairway)	tangga	[taŋga]
mailbox	kotak pos	[kotaʔ pos]
garbage can	tong sampah	[toŋ sampah]
elevator	elevator	[elevator]

electricity	listrik	[listriʔ]
light bulb	bohlam	[bohlam]
switch	sakelar	[sakelar]
wall socket	colokan	[tʃolokan]
fuse	sekering	[sekeriŋ]

door	pintu	[pintu]
handle, doorknob	gagang pintu	[gagaŋ pintu]
key	kunci	[kuntʃi]
doormat	tikar	[tikar]

door lock	kunci pintu	[kuntʃi pintu]
doorbell	bel	[bel]
knock (at the door)	ketukan	[ketukan]
to knock (vi)	mengetuk	[meŋetuʔ]
peephole	lubang intip	[lubaŋ intip]

yard	pekarangan	[pekaraŋan]
garden	kebun	[kebun]
swimming pool	kolam renang	[kolam renaŋ]
gym (home gym)	gym	[dʒim]
tennis court	lapangan tenis	[lapaŋan tenis]
garage	garasi	[garasi]

| private property | milik pribadi | [miliʔ pribadi] |
| warning sign | tanda peringatan | [tanda periŋatan] |

security	keamanan	[keamanan]
security guard	satpam, pengawal	[satpam], [peŋawal]
renovations	renovasi	[renovasi]
to renovate (vt)	merenovasi	[merenovasi]
to put in order	membereskan	[membereskan]
to paint (~ a wall)	mengecat	[məŋetʃat]
wallpaper	kertas dinding	[kertas dindiŋ]
to varnish (vt)	memernis	[memernis]
pipe	pipa	[pipa]
tools	peralatan	[pəralatan]
basement	rubanah	[rubanah]
sewerage (system)	riol	[riol]

14. House. Apartment. Part 2

apartment	apartemen	[apartemen]
room	kamar	[kamar]
bedroom	kamar tidur	[kamar tidur]
dining room	ruang makan	[ruaŋ makan]
living room	ruang tamu	[ruaŋ tamu]
study (home office)	ruang kerja	[ruaŋ kerdʒ/a]
entry room	ruang depan	[ruaŋ depan]
bathroom (room with a bath or shower)	kamar mandi	[kamar mandi]
half bath	kamar kecil	[kamar ketʃil]
floor	lantai	[lantaj]
ceiling	plafon, langit-langit	[plafon], [laŋit-laŋit]
to dust (vt)	menyapu debu	[mənjapu debu]
vacuum cleaner	pengisap debu	[peŋisap debu]
to vacuum (vt)	membersihkan dengan pengisap debu	[membersihkan deŋan peŋisap debu]
mop	kain pel	[kain pel]
dust cloth	lap	[lap]
short broom	sapu lidi	[sapu lidi]
dustpan	pengki	[peŋki]
furniture	mebel	[mebel]
table	meja	[medʒ/a]
chair	kursi	[kursi]
armchair	kursi malas	[kursi malas]
bookcase	lemari buku	[lemari buku]
shelf	rak	[ra']
wardrobe	lemari pakaian	[lemari pakajan]

mirror	**cermin**	[tʃermin]
carpet	**permadani**	[pərmadani]
fireplace	**perapian**	[pərapian]
drapes	**gorden**	[gorden]
table lamp	**lampu meja**	[lampu medʒia]
chandelier	**lampu bercabang**	[lampu bərtʃabaŋ]

kitchen	**dapur**	[dapur]
gas stove (range)	**kompor gas**	[kompor gas]
electric stove	**kompor listrik**	[kompor listriʔ]
microwave oven	**microwave**	[majkrowav]

refrigerator	**lemari es, kulkas**	[lemari es], [kulkas]
freezer	**lemari pembeku**	[lemari pembeku]
dishwasher	**mesin pencuci piring**	[mesin pentʃutʃi piriŋ]
faucet	**keran**	[keran]

meat grinder	**alat pelumat daging**	[alat pelumat dagiŋ]
juicer	**mesin sari buah**	[mesin sari buah]
toaster	**alat pemanggang roti**	[alat pemaŋgaŋ roti]
mixer	**pencampur**	[pentʃampur]

coffee machine	**mesin pembuat kopi**	[mesin pembuat kopi]
kettle	**cerek**	[tʃereʔ]
teapot	**teko**	[teko]

TV set	**pesawat TV**	[pesawat ti-vi]
VCR (video recorder)	**video, VCR**	[vidio], [vi-si-er]
iron (e.g., steam ~)	**setrika**	[setrika]
telephone	**telepon**	[telepon]

15. Professions. Social status

director	**direktur**	[direktur]
superior	**atasan**	[atasan]
president	**presiden**	[presiden]
assistant	**asisten**	[asisten]
secretary	**sekretaris**	[sekretaris]

owner, proprietor	**pemilik**	[pemiliʔ]
partner	**mitra**	[mitra]
stockholder	**pemegang saham**	[pemegaŋ saham]

businessman	**pengusaha, pebisnis**	[peŋusaha], [pebisnis]
millionaire	**jutawan**	[dʒiutawan]
billionaire	**miliarder**	[miliarder]

actor	**aktor**	[aktor]
architect	**arsitek**	[arsiteʔ]
banker	**bankir**	[bankir]

broker	broker, pialang	[broker], [pialaŋ]
veterinarian	dokter hewan	[dokter hewan]
doctor	dokter	[dokter]
chambermaid	pelayan kamar	[pelajan kamar]
designer	desainer, perancang	[desajner], [pərantʃaŋ]
correspondent	koresponden	[koresponden]
delivery man	kurir	[kurir]

electrician	tukang listrik	[tukaŋ listriʔ]
musician	musisi, musikus	[musisi], [musikus]
babysitter	pengasuh anak	[peŋasuh anaʔ]
hairdresser	tukang cukur	[tukaŋ tʃukur]
herder, shepherd	penggembala	[peŋgembala]

singer (masc.)	biduan	[biduan]
translator	penerjemah	[penerdʒˈemah]
writer	penulis	[penulis]
carpenter	tukang kayu	[tukaŋ kaju]
cook	koki, juru masak	[koki], [dʒˈuru masaʔ]

fireman	pemadam kebakaran	[pemadam kebakaran]
police officer	polisi	[polisi]
mailman	tukang pos	[tukaŋ pos]
programmer	pemrogram	[pemrogram]
salesman (store staff)	pramuniaga	[pramuniaga]

worker	buruh, pekerja	[buruh], [pekerdʒˈa]
gardener	tukang kebun	[tukaŋ kebun]
plumber	tukang pipa	[tukaŋ pipa]
dentist	dokter gigi	[dokter gigi]
flight attendant (fem.)	pramugari	[pramugari]

dancer (masc.)	penari lelaki	[penari lelaki]
bodyguard	pengawal pribadi	[peŋawal pribadi]
scientist	ilmuwan	[ilmuwan]
schoolteacher	guru	[guru]

farmer	petani	[petani]
surgeon	dokter bedah	[dokter bedah]
miner	penambang	[penambaŋ]
chef (kitchen chef)	koki kepala	[koki kepala]
driver	sopir	[sopir]

16. Sport

kind of sports	jenis olahraga	[dʒˈenis olahraga]
soccer	sepak bola	[sepaʔ bola]
hockey	hoki	[hoki]
basketball	bola basket	[bola basket]
baseball	bisbol	[bisbol]

volleyball	**bola voli**	[bola voli]
boxing	**tinju**	[tindʒʲu]
wrestling	**gulat**	[gulat]
tennis	**tenis**	[tenis]
swimming	**berenang**	[bərenaŋ]

chess	**catur**	[tʃatur]
running	**lari**	[lari]
athletics	**atletik**	[atletiʔ]
figure skating	**seluncur indah**	[seluntʃur indah]
cycling	**bersepeda**	[bərsepeda]

billiards	**biliar**	[biliar]
bodybuilding	**binaraga**	[binaraga]
golf	**golf**	[golf]
scuba diving	**selam skuba**	[selam skuba]
sailing	**berlayar**	[bərlajar]
archery	**memanah**	[memanah]

period, half	**babak**	[babaʔ]
half-time	**waktu istirahat**	[waktu istirahat]
tie	**seri, hasil imbang**	[seri], [hasil imbaŋ]
to tie (vi)	**bermain seri**	[bərmajn seri]

treadmill	**treadmill**	[tredmil]
player	**pemain**	[pemajn]
substitute	**pemain pengganti**	[pemajn peŋganti]
substitutes bench	**bangku pemain pengganti**	[baŋku pemajn peŋganti]

match	**pertandingan**	[pərtandiŋan]
goal	**gawang**	[gawaŋ]
goalkeeper	**kiper, penjaga gawang**	[kiper], [pendʒʲaga gawaŋ]
goal (score)	**gol**	[gol]

Olympic Games	**Olimpiade**	[olimpiade]
to set a record	**menciptakan rekor**	[məntʃiptakan rekor]
final	**final**	[final]
champion	**juara**	[dʒʲuara]
championship	**kejuaraan**	[kedʒʲuaraʔan]

winner	**pemenang**	[pemenaŋ]
victory	**kemenangan**	[kemenaŋan]
to win (vi)	**menang**	[menaŋ]
to lose (not win)	**kalah**	[kalah]
medal	**medali**	[medali]

first place	**tempat pertama**	[tempat pərtama]
second place	**tempat kedua**	[tempat kedua]
third place	**tempat ketiga**	[tempat ketiga]
stadium	**stadion**	[stadion]
fan, supporter	**pendukung**	[pendukuŋ]

| trainer, coach | pelatih | [pelatih] |
| training | latihan | [latihan] |

17. Foreign languages. Orthography

language	bahasa	[bahasa]
to study (vt)	mempelajari	[mempeladʒʲari]
pronunciation	pelafalan	[pelafalan]
accent	aksen	[aksen]

noun	nomina	[nomina]
adjective	adjektiva	[adʒʲektiva]
verb	verba	[verba]
adverb	adverbia	[adverbia]

pronoun	kata ganti	[kata ganti]
interjection	kata seru	[kata seru]
preposition	preposisi, kata depan	[preposisi], [kata depan]

root	kata dasar	[kata dasar]
ending	akhiran	[ahiran]
prefix	prefiks, awalan	[prefiks], [awalan]
syllable	suku kata	[suku kata]
suffix	sufiks, akhiran	[sufiks], [ahiran]

stress mark	tanda tekanan	[tanda tekanan]
period, dot	titik	[titiʔ]
comma	koma	[koma]
colon	titik dua	[titiʔ dua]
ellipsis	elipsis, lesapan	[elipsis], [lesapan]

question	pertanyaan	[pərtanjaʔan]
question mark	tanda tanya	[tanda tanja]
exclamation point	tanda seru	[tanda seru]

in quotation marks	dalam tanda petik	[dalam tanda petiʔ]
in parenthesis	dalam tanda kurung	[dalam tanda kuruŋ]
letter	huruf	[huruf]
capital letter	huruf kapital	[huruf kapital]

sentence	kalimat	[kalimat]
group of words	rangkaian kata	[raŋkajan kata]
expression	ungkapan	[uŋkapan]

subject	subjek	[subdʒʲeʔ]
predicate	predikat	[predikat]
line	baris	[baris]
paragraph	alinea, paragraf	[alinea], [paragraf]
synonym	sinonim	[sinonim]
antonym	antonim	[antonim]

exception	**perkecualian**	[pərketʃualian]
to underline (vt)	**menggaris bawahi**	[məŋgaris bawahi]
rules	**peraturan**	[pəraturan]
grammar	**tatabahasa**	[tatabahasa]
vocabulary	**kosakata**	[kosakata]
phonetics	**fonetik**	[fonetiʔ]
alphabet	**alfabet, abjad**	[alfabet], [abdʒʲad]
textbook	**buku pelajaran**	[buku peladʒʲaran]
dictionary	**kamus**	[kamus]
phrasebook	**panduan percakapan**	[panduan pərtʃakapan]
word	**kata**	[kata]
meaning	**arti**	[arti]
memory	**memori, daya ingat**	[memori], [daja iŋat]

18. The Earth. Geography

the Earth	**Bumi**	[bumi]
the globe (the Earth)	**bola Bumi**	[bola bumi]
planet	**planet**	[planet]
geography	**geografi**	[geografi]
nature	**alam**	[alam]
map	**peta**	[peta]
atlas	**atlas**	[atlas]
in the north	**di utara**	[di utara]
in the south	**di selatan**	[di selatan]
in the west	**di barat**	[di barat]
in the east	**di timur**	[di timur]
sea	**laut**	[laut]
ocean	**samudra**	[samudra]
gulf (bay)	**teluk**	[teluʔ]
straits	**selat**	[selat]
continent (mainland)	**benua**	[benua]
island	**pulau**	[pulau]
peninsula	**semenanjung, jazirah**	[semenandʒʲuŋ], [dʒʲazirah]
archipelago	**kepulauan**	[kepulauan]
harbor	**pelabuhan**	[pelabuhan]
coral reef	**terumbu karang**	[tərumbu karaŋ]
shore	**pantai**	[pantaj]
coast	**pantai**	[pantaj]
flow (flood tide)	**air pasang**	[air pasaŋ]
ebb (ebb tide)	**air surut**	[air surut]

latitude	lintang	[lintaŋ]
longitude	garis bujur	[garis budʒ'ur]
parallel	sejajar	[sedʒ'adʒ'ar]
equator	khatulistiwa	[hatulistiwa]

sky	langit	[laŋit]
horizon	horizon	[horizon]
atmosphere	atmosfer	[atmosfer]

mountain	gunung	[gunuŋ]
summit, top	puncak	[puntʃaʔ]
cliff	tebing	[tebiŋ]
hill	bukit	[bukit]

volcano	gunung api	[gunuŋ api]
glacier	gletser	[gletser]
waterfall	air terjun	[air tərdʒ'un]
plain	dataran	[dataran]

river	sungai	[suŋaj]
spring (natural source)	mata air	[mata air]
bank (of river)	tebing sungai	[tebiŋ suŋaj]
downstream (adv)	ke hilir	[ke hilir]
upstream (adv)	ke hulu	[ke hulu]

lake	danau	[danau]
dam	dam, bendungan	[dam], [benduŋan]
canal	kanal, terusan	[kanal], [tərusan]
swamp (marshland)	rawa	[rawa]
ice	es	[es]

19. Countries of the world. Part 1

Europe	Eropa	[eropa]
European Union	Uni Eropa	[uni eropa]
European (n)	orang Eropa	[oraŋ eropa]
European (adj)	Eropa	[eropa]

Austria	Austria	[austria]
Great Britain	Britania Raya	[britania raja]
England	Inggris	[iŋgris]
Belgium	Belgia	[belgia]
Germany	Jerman	[dʒ'erman]

Netherlands	Belanda	[belanda]
Holland	Belanda	[belanda]
Greece	Yunani	[yunani]
Denmark	Denmark	[denmarʔ]
Ireland	Irlandia	[irlandia]
Iceland	Islandia	[islandia]

Spain	**Spanyol**	[spanjol]
Italy	**Italia**	[italia]
Cyprus	**Siprus**	[siprus]
Malta	**Malta**	[malta]
Norway	**Norwegia**	[norwegia]
Portugal	**Portugal**	[portugal]
Finland	**Finlandia**	[finlandia]
France	**Prancis**	[prantʃis]
Sweden	**Swedia**	[swedia]
Switzerland	**Swiss**	[swiss]
Scotland	**Skotlandia**	[skotlandia]
Vatican	**Vatikan**	[vatikan]
Liechtenstein	**Liechtenstein**	[lajhtensteyn]
Luxembourg	**Luksemburg**	[luksemburg]
Monaco	**Monako**	[monako]
Albania	**Albania**	[albania]
Bulgaria	**Bulgaria**	[bulgaria]
Hungary	**Hongaria**	[honjaria]
Latvia	**Latvia**	[latvia]
Lithuania	**Lituania**	[lituania]
Poland	**Polandia**	[polandia]
Romania	**Romania**	[romania]
Serbia	**Serbia**	[serbia]
Slovakia	**Slowakia**	[slowakia]
Croatia	**Kroasia**	[kroasia]
Czech Republic	**Republik Ceko**	[republi' tʃeko]
Estonia	**Estonia**	[estonia]
Bosnia and Herzegovina	**Bosnia-Hercegovina**	[bosnia-hersegovina]
Macedonia (Republic of ~)	**Makedonia**	[makedonia]
Slovenia	**Slovenia**	[slovenia]
Montenegro	**Montenegro**	[montenegro]
Belarus	**Belarusia**	[belarusia]
Moldova, Moldavia	**Moldova**	[moldova]
Russia	**Rusia**	[rusia]
Ukraine	**Ukraina**	[ukrajna]

20. Countries of the world. Part 2

Asia	**Asia**	[asia]
Vietnam	**Vietnam**	[vjetnam]
India	**India**	[india]
Israel	**Israel**	[israel]
China	**Tiongkok**	[tjonko']
Lebanon	**Lebanon**	[lebanon]

Mongolia	**Mongolia**	[moŋolia]
Malaysia	**Malaysia**	[malajsia]
Pakistan	**Pakistan**	[pakistan]
Saudi Arabia	**Arab Saudi**	[arab saudi]
Thailand	**Thailand**	[tajland]
Taiwan	**Taiwan**	[tajwan]
Turkey	**Turki**	[turki]
Japan	**Jepang**	[dʒʲepaŋ]
Afghanistan	**Afghanistan**	[afganistan]
Bangladesh	**Bangladesh**	[baŋladeʃ]
Indonesia	**Indonesia**	[indonesia]
Jordan	**Yordania**	[yordania]
Iraq	**Irak**	[iraʔ]
Iran	**Iran**	[iran]
Cambodia	**Kamboja**	[kambodʒʲa]
Kuwait	**Kuwait**	[kuweyt]
Laos	**Laos**	[laos]
Myanmar	**Myanmar**	[myanmar]
Nepal	**Nepal**	[nepal]
United Arab Emirates	**Uni Emirat Arab**	[uni emirat arab]
Syria	**Suriah**	[suriah]
Palestine	**Palestina**	[palestina]
South Korea	**Korea Selatan**	[korea selatan]
North Korea	**Korea Utara**	[korea utara]
United States of America	**Amerika Serikat**	[amerika serikat]
Canada	**Kanada**	[kanada]
Mexico	**Meksiko**	[meksiko]
Argentina	**Argentina**	[argentina]
Brazil	**Brasil**	[brasil]
Colombia	**Kolombia**	[kolombia]
Cuba	**Kuba**	[kuba]
Chile	**Chili**	[tʃili]
Venezuela	**Venezuela**	[venezuela]
Ecuador	**Ekuador**	[ekuador]
The Bahamas	**Kepulauan Bahama**	[kepulauan bahama]
Panama	**Panama**	[panama]
Egypt	**Mesir**	[mesir]
Morocco	**Maroko**	[maroko]
Tunisia	**Tunisia**	[tunisia]
Kenya	**Kenya**	[kenia]
Libya	**Libia**	[libia]
South Africa	**Afrika Selatan**	[afrika selatan]
Australia	**Australia**	[australia]
New Zealand	**Selandia Baru**	[selandia baru]

21. Weather. Natural disasters

weather	cuaca	[tʃuatʃa]
weather forecast	prakiraan cuaca	[prakira'an tʃuatʃa]
temperature	temperatur, suhu	[temperatur], [suhu]
thermometer	termometer	[termometər]
barometer	barometer	[barometer]

sun	matahari	[matahari]
to shine (vi)	bersinar	[bərsinar]
sunny (day)	cerah	[tʃerah]
to come up (vi)	terbit	[terbit]
to set (vi)	terbenam	[terbenam]

rain	hujan	[hudʒian]
it's raining	hujan turun	[hudʒian turun]
pouring rain	hujan lebat	[hudʒian lebat]
rain cloud	awan mendung	[awan menduŋ]
puddle	kubangan	[kubaŋan]
to get wet (in rain)	kehujanan	[kehudʒianan]

thunderstorm	hujan badai	[hudʒian badaj]
lightning (~ strike)	kilat	[kilat]
to flash (vi)	berkilau	[bərkilau]
thunder	petir	[petir]
it's thundering	bergemuruh	[bərgemuruh]
hail	hujan es	[hudʒian es]
it's hailing	hujan es	[hudʒian es]

heat (extreme ~)	panas, gerah	[panas], [gerah]
it's hot	panas	[panas]
it's warm	hangat	[haŋat]
it's cold	dingin	[diŋin]

fog (mist)	kabut	[kabut]
foggy	berkabut	[bərkabut]
cloud	awan	[awan]
cloudy (adj)	berawan	[bərawan]
humidity	kelembapan	[kelembapan]

snow	salju	[saldʒiu]
it's snowing	turun salju	[turun saldʒiu]
frost (severe ~, freezing cold)	dingin	[diŋin]
below zero (adv)	di bawah nol	[di bawah nol]
hoarfrost	embun beku	[embun beku]

bad weather	cuaca buruk	[tʃuatʃa buru']
disaster	bencana	[bentʃana]
flood, inundation	banjir	[bandʒir]
avalanche	longsor	[loŋsor]

earthquake	gempa bumi	[gempa bumi]
tremor, quake	gempa	[gempa]
epicenter	episentrum	[episentrum]
eruption	erupsi, letusan	[erupsi], [letusan]
lava	lava, lahar	[lava], [lahar]
tornado	tornado	[tornado]
twister	puting beliung	[putiŋ beliuŋ]
hurricane	topan	[topan]
tsunami	tsunami	[tsunami]
cyclone	siklon	[siklon]

22. Animals. Part 1

animal	binatang	[binataŋ]
predator	predator, pemangsa	[predator], [pemaŋsa]
tiger	harimau	[harimau]
lion	singa	[siŋa]
wolf	serigala	[serigala]
fox	rubah	[rubah]
jaguar	jaguar	[dʒʲaguar]
lynx	lynx	[links]
coyote	koyote	[koyot]
jackal	jakal	[dʒʲakal]
hyena	hiena	[hiena]
squirrel	bajing	[badʒiŋ]
hedgehog	landak susu	[landaʔ susu]
rabbit	kelinci	[kelintʃi]
raccoon	rakun	[rakun]
hamster	hamster	[hamster]
mole	tikus mondok	[tikus mondoʔ]
mouse	tikus	[tikus]
rat	tikus besar	[tikus besar]
bat	kelelawar	[kelelawar]
beaver	beaver	[beaver]
horse	kuda	[kuda]
deer	rusa	[rusa]
camel	unta	[unta]
zebra	kuda belang	[kuda belaŋ]
whale	ikan paus	[ikan paus]
seal	anjing laut	[andʒiŋ laut]
walrus	walrus	[walrus]
dolphin	lumba-lumba	[lumba-lumba]
bear	beruang	[bəruaŋ]

monkey	**monyet**	[monjet]
elephant	**gajah**	[gadʒʲah]
rhinoceros	**badak**	[badaʔ]
giraffe	**jerapah**	[dʒʲerapah]

hippopotamus	**kuda nil**	[kuda nil]
kangaroo	**kanguru**	[kaŋuru]
cat	**kucing betina**	[kutʃiŋ betina]
dog	**anjing**	[andʒiŋ]

cow	**sapi**	[sapi]
bull	**sapi jantan**	[sapi dʒʲantan]
sheep (ewe)	**domba**	[domba]
goat	**kambing betina**	[kambiŋ betina]

donkey	**keledai**	[keledaj]
pig, hog	**babi**	[babi]
hen (chicken)	**ayam betina**	[ajam betina]
rooster	**ayam jago**	[ajam dʒʲago]

duck	**bebek**	[bebeʔ]
goose	**angsa**	[aŋsa]
turkey (hen)	**kalkun betina**	[kalkun betina]
sheepdog	**anjing gembala**	[andʒiŋ gembala]

23. Animals. Part 2

bird	**burung**	[buruŋ]
pigeon	**burung dara**	[buruŋ dara]
sparrow	**burung gereja**	[buruŋ geredʒʲa]
tit (great tit)	**burung tit**	[buruŋ tit]
magpie	**burung murai**	[buruŋ muraj]

eagle	**rajawali**	[radʒʲawali]
hawk	**elang**	[elaŋ]
falcon	**alap-alap**	[alap-alap]

swan	**angsa**	[aŋsa]
crane	**burung jenjang**	[buruŋ dʒʲendʒʲaŋ]
stork	**bangau**	[baŋau]
parrot	**burung nuri**	[buruŋ nuri]
peacock	**burung merak**	[buruŋ meraʔ]
ostrich	**burung unta**	[buruŋ unta]

heron	**kuntul**	[kuntul]
nightingale	**burung bulbul**	[buruŋ bulbul]
swallow	**burung walet**	[buruŋ walet]
woodpecker	**burung pelatuk**	[buruŋ pelatuʔ]
cuckoo	**burung kukuk**	[buruŋ kukuʔ]
owl	**burung hantu**	[buruŋ hantu]

penguin	penguin	[peŋuin]
tuna	tuna	[tuna]
trout	ikan forel	[ikan forel]
eel	belut	[belut]
shark	ikan hiu	[ikan hiu]
crab	kepiting	[kepitiŋ]
jellyfish	ubur-ubur	[ubur-ubur]
octopus	gurita	[gurita]
starfish	bintang laut	[bintaŋ laut]
sea urchin	landak laut	[landaʾ laut]
seahorse	kuda laut	[kuda laut]
shrimp	udang	[udaŋ]
snake	ular	[ular]
viper	ular viper	[ular viper]
lizard	kadal	[kadal]
iguana	iguana	[iguana]
chameleon	bunglon	[buŋlon]
scorpion	kalajengking	[kaladʒʲeŋkiŋ]
turtle	kura-kura	[kura-kura]
frog	katak	[kataʾ]
crocodile	buaya	[buaja]
insect, bug	serangga	[seraŋga]
butterfly	kupu-kupu	[kupu-kupu]
ant	semut	[semut]
fly	lalat	[lalat]
mosquito	nyamuk	[njamuʾ]
beetle	kumbang	[kumbaŋ]
bee	lebah	[lebah]
spider	laba-laba	[laba-laba]

24. Trees. Plants

tree	pohon	[pohon]
birch	pohon berk	[pohon bərʾ]
oak	pohon eik	[pohon eiʾ]
linden tree	pohon linden	[pohon linden]
aspen	pohon aspen	[pohon aspen]
maple	pohon mapel	[pohon mapel]
spruce	pohon den	[pohon den]
pine	pohon pinus	[pohon pinus]
cedar	pohon aras	[pohon aras]
poplar	pohon poplar	[pohon poplar]
rowan	pohon rowan	[pohon rowan]

beech	**pohon nothofagus**	[pohon notofagus]
elm	**pohon elm**	[pohon elm]
ash (tree)	**pohon abu**	[pohon abu]
chestnut	**kastanye**	[kastanje]
palm tree	**palem**	[palem]
bush	**rumpun**	[rumpun]
mushroom	**jamur**	[dʒamur]
poisonous mushroom	**jamur beracun**	[dʒamur bəratʃun]
cep (Boletus edulis)	**jamur boletus**	[dʒamur boletus]
russula	**jamur rusula**	[dʒamur rusula]
fly agaric	**jamur Amanita muscaria**	[dʒamur amanita mustʃaria]
death cap	**jamur topi kematian**	[dʒamur topi kematian]
flower	**bunga**	[buŋa]
bouquet (of flowers)	**buket**	[buket]
rose (flower)	**mawar**	[mawar]
tulip	**tulip**	[tulip]
carnation	**bunga anyelir**	[buŋa anjelir]
camomile	**bunga margrit**	[buŋa margrit]
cactus	**kaktus**	[kaktus]
lily of the valley	**lili lembah**	[lili lembah]
snowdrop	**bunga tetesan salju**	[buŋa tetesan saldʒu]
water lily	**lili air**	[lili air]
greenhouse (tropical ~)	**rumah kaca**	[rumah katʃa]
lawn	**halaman berumput**	[halaman bərumput]
flowerbed	**bedeng bunga**	[bedeŋ buŋa]
plant	**tumbuhan**	[tumbuhan]
grass	**rumput**	[rumput]
leaf	**daun**	[daun]
petal	**kelopak**	[kelopaʔ]
stem	**batang**	[bataŋ]
young plant (shoot)	**tunas**	[tunas]
cereal crops	**padi-padian**	[padi-padian]
wheat	**gandum**	[gandum]
rye	**gandum hitam**	[gandum hitam]
oats	**oat**	[oat]
millet	**jawawut**	[dʒawawut]
barley	**jelai**	[dʒelaj]
corn	**jagung**	[dʒaguŋ]
rice	**beras**	[beras]

25. Various useful words

balance (of situation)	**keseimbangan**	[keseimbaŋan]
base (basis)	**basis, dasar**	[basis], [dasar]
beginning	**permulaan**	[pərmula'an]
category	**kategori**	[kategori]
choice	**pilihan**	[pilihan]
coincidence	**kebetulan**	[kebetulan]
comparison	**perbandingan**	[pərbandiŋan]
degree (extent, amount)	**tingkat**	[tiŋkat]
development	**perkembangan**	[pərkembaŋan]
difference	**perbedaan**	[pərbeda'an]
effect (e.g., of drugs)	**efek, pengaruh**	[efek], [peŋaruh]
effort (exertion)	**usaha**	[usaha]
element	**unsur**	[unsur]
example (illustration)	**contoh**	[ʧontoh]
fact	**fakta**	[fakta]
help	**bantuan**	[bantuan]
ideal	**ideal**	[ideal]
kind (sort, type)	**jenis**	[ʤʲenis]
mistake, error	**kesalahan**	[kesalahan]
moment	**saat, waktu**	[sa'at], [waktu]
obstacle	**rintangan**	[rintaŋan]
part (~ of sth)	**bagian**	[bagian]
pause (break)	**istirahat**	[istirahat]
position	**posisi**	[posisi]
problem	**masalah**	[masalah]
process	**proses**	[proses]
progress	**kemajuan**	[kemaʤʲuan]
property (quality)	**sifat**	[sifat]
reaction	**reaksi**	[reaksi]
risk	**risiko**	[risiko]
secret	**rahasia**	[rahasia]
series	**rangkaian**	[raŋkajan]
shape (outer form)	**bentuk, rupa**	[bentuk], [rupa]
situation	**situasi**	[situasi]
solution	**solusi, penyelesaian**	[solusi], [penjelesajan]
standard (adj)	**standar**	[standar]
stop (pause)	**perhentian**	[pərhentian]
style	**gaya**	[gaja]
system	**sistem**	[sistem]

table (chart)	**tabel**	[tabel]
tempo, rate	**tempo, laju**	[tempo], [ladʒˑu]
term (word, expression)	**istilah**	[istilah]
truth (e.g., moment of ~)	**kebenaran**	[kebenaran]
turn (please wait your ~)	**giliran**	[giliran]
urgent (adj)	**segera**	[segera]
utility (usefulness)	**kegunaan**	[keguna'an]
variant (alternative)	**varian**	[varian]
way (means, method)	**cara**	[tʃara]
zone	**zona**	[zona]

26. Modifiers. Adjectives. Part 1

additional (adj)	**tambahan**	[tambahan]
ancient (~ civilization)	**kuno**	[kuno]
artificial (adj)	**buatan**	[buatan]
bad (adj)	**buruk, jelek**	[buruk], [dʒˑele']
beautiful (person)	**cantik**	[tʃanti']
big (in size)	**besar**	[besar]
bitter (taste)	**pahit**	[pahit]
blind (sightless)	**buta**	[buta]
central (adj)	**sentral**	[sentral]
children's (adj)	**kanak-kanak**	[kana'-kana']
clandestine (secret)	**rahasia, diam-diam**	[rahasia], [diam-diam]
clean (free from dirt)	**bersih**	[bərsih]
clever (smart)	**pandai, pintar**	[pandaj], [pintar]
compatible (adj)	**serasi, cocok**	[serasi], [tʃotʃo']
contented (satisfied)	**puas**	[puas]
dangerous (adj)	**berbahaya**	[bərbahaja]
dead (not alive)	**mati**	[mati]
dense (fog, smoke)	**pekat**	[pekat]
difficult (decision)	**sukar, sulit**	[sukar], [sulit]
dirty (not clean)	**kotor**	[kotor]
easy (not difficult)	**mudah**	[mudah]
empty (glass, room)	**kosong**	[koson]
exact (amount)	**tepat**	[tepat]
excellent (adj)	**sangat baik**	[saŋat bai']
excessive (adj)	**berlebihan**	[bərlebihan]
exterior (adj)	**luar**	[luar]
fast (quick)	**cepat**	[tʃepat]
fertile (land, soil)	**subur**	[subur]
fragile (china, glass)	**rapuh**	[rapuh]
free (at no cost)	**gratis**	[gratis]

fresh (~ water)	**tawar**	[tawar]
frozen (food)	**beku**	[beku]
full (completely filled)	**penuh**	[penuh]
happy (adj)	**bahagia**	[bahagia]
hard (not soft)	**keras**	[keras]
huge (adj)	**sangat besar**	[saŋat besar]
ill (sick, unwell)	**sakit**	[sakit]
immobile (adj)	**tak bergerak**	[ta' bərgera']
important (adj)	**penting**	[pentiŋ]
interior (adj)	**dalam**	[dalam]
last (e.g., ~ week)	**lalu**	[lalu]
last (final)	**terakhir**	[tərahir]
left (e.g., ~ side)	**kiri**	[kiri]
legal (legitimate)	**sah**	[sah]
light (in weight)	**ringan**	[riŋan]
liquid (fluid)	**cair**	[ʧair]
long (e.g., ~ hair)	**panjang**	[panʤ¡aŋ]
loud (voice, etc.)	**lantang**	[lantaŋ]
low (voice)	**lirih**	[lirih]

27. Modifiers. Adjectives. Part 2

main (principal)	**utama**	[utama]
matt, matte	**kusam**	[kusam]
mysterious (adj)	**misterius**	[misterius]
narrow (street, etc.)	**sempit**	[sempit]
native (~ country)	**asli**	[asli]
negative (~ response)	**negatif**	[negatif]
new (adj)	**baru**	[baru]
next (e.g., ~ week)	**depan**	[depan]
normal (adj)	**normal**	[normal]
not difficult (adj)	**tidak sukar**	[tida' sukar]
obligatory (adj)	**wajib**	[waʤib]
old (house)	**tua**	[tua]
open (adj)	**terbuka**	[tərbuka]
opposite (adj)	**bertentangan**	[bərtentaŋan]
ordinary (usual)	**biasa**	[biasa]
original (unusual)	**orisinal, asli**	[orisinal], [asli]
personal (adj)	**pribadi**	[pribadi]
polite (adj)	**sopan**	[sopan]
poor (not rich)	**miskin**	[miskin]
possible (adj)	**mungkin**	[muŋkin]
principal (main)	**utama**	[utama]

probable (adj)	**mungkin**	[muŋkin]
prolonged (e.g., ~ applause)	**panjang**	[pandʒiaŋ]
public (open to all)	**umum**	[umum]
rare (adj)	**jarang**	[dʒiaraŋ]
raw (uncooked)	**mentah**	[məntah]
right (not left)	**kanan**	[kanan]
ripe (fruit)	**masak**	[masaʔ]
risky (adj)	**riskan**	[riskan]
sad (~ look)	**sedih**	[sedih]
second hand (adj)	**bekas**	[bekas]
shallow (water)	**dangkal**	[daŋkal]
sharp (blade, etc.)	**tajam**	[tadʒiam]
short (in length)	**pendek**	[pendeʔ]
similar (adj)	**mirip**	[mirip]
small (in size)	**kecil**	[ketʃil]
smooth (surface)	**rata, halus**	[rata], [halus]
soft (~ toys)	**empuk**	[empuʔ]
solid (~ wall)	**kuat, kukuh**	[kuat], [kukuh]
sour (flavor, taste)	**masam**	[masam]
spacious (house, etc.)	**lapang, luas**	[lapaŋ], [luas]
special (adj)	**khusus**	[husus]
straight (line, road)	**lurus**	[lurus]
strong (person)	**kuat**	[kuat]
stupid (foolish)	**bodoh**	[bodoh]
superb, perfect (adj)	**cemerlang**	[tʃemerlaŋ]
sweet (sugary)	**manis**	[manis]
tan (adj)	**hitam terbakar matahari**	[hitam tərbakar matahari]
tasty (delicious)	**enak**	[enaʔ]
unclear (adj)	**tidak jelas**	[tidaʔ dʒielas]

28. Verbs. Part 1

to accuse (vt)	**menuduh**	[mənuduh]
to agree (say yes)	**setuju**	[setudʒiu]
to announce (vt)	**mengumumkan**	[məŋumumkan]
to answer (vi, vt)	**menjawab**	[məndʒiawab]
to apologize (vi)	**meminta maaf**	[meminta maʔaf]
to arrive (vi)	**datang**	[dataŋ]
to ask (~ oneself)	**bertanya**	[bərtanja]
to be absent	**absen, tidak hadir**	[absen], [tidaʔ hadir]
to be afraid	**takut**	[takut]
to be born	**lahir**	[lahir]

to be in a hurry	tergesa-gesa	[tərgesa-gesa]
to beat (to hit)	memukul	[memukul]
to begin (vt)	memulai, membuka	[memulaj], [membuka]
to believe (in God)	percaya	[pərtʃaja]
to belong to …	kepunyaan …	[kepunjaʔan …]
to break (split into pieces)	memecahkan	[memetʃahkan]
to build (vt)	membangun	[membaŋun]
to buy (purchase)	membeli	[membeli]
can (v aux)	bisa	[bisa]
can (v aux)	bisa	[bisa]
to cancel (call off)	membatalkan	[membatalkan]
to catch (vt)	menangkap	[mənaŋkap]
to change (vt)	mengubah	[məŋubah]
to check (to examine)	memeriksa	[memeriksa]
to choose (select)	memilih	[memilih]
to clean up (tidy)	membereskan	[membereskan]
to close (vt)	menutup	[mənutup]
to compare (vt)	membandingkan	[membandiŋkan]
to complain (vi, vt)	mengeluh	[məŋeluh]
to confirm (vt)	mengonfirmasi	[məŋonfirmasi]
to congratulate (vt)	mengucapkan selamat	[məŋutʃapkan selamat]
to cook (dinner)	memasak	[memasaʔ]
to copy (vt)	menyalin	[mənjalin]
to cost (vt)	berharga	[bərharga]
to count (add up)	menghitung	[məŋhituŋ]
to count on …	mengharapkan …	[məŋharapkan …]
to create (vt)	menciptakan	[məntʃiptakan]
to cry (weep)	menangis	[mənaŋis]
to dance (vi, vt)	berdansa, menari	[bərdansa], [menari]
to deceive (vi, vt)	menipu	[mənipu]
to decide (~ to do sth)	memutuskan	[memutuskan]
to delete (vt)	menghapus	[məŋhapus]
to demand (request firmly)	menuntut	[mənuntut]
to deny (vt)	memungkiri	[memuŋkiri]
to depend on …	tergantung pada …	[tərgantuŋ pada …]
to despise (vt)	benci, membenci	[bentʃi], [membentʃi]
to die (vi)	mati, meninggal	[mati], [meniŋgal]
to dig (vt)	menggali	[məŋgali]
to disappear (vi)	menghilang	[məŋhilaŋ]
to discuss (vt)	membicarakan	[membitʃarakan]
to disturb (vt)	mengganggu	[məŋgaŋgu]

29. Verbs. Part 2

to dive (vi)	**menyelam**	[mənjelam]
to divorce (vi)	**bercerai**	[bərtʃeraj]
to do (vt)	**membuat**	[membuat]
to doubt (have doubts)	**ragu-ragu**	[ragu-ragu]
to drink (vi, vt)	**minum**	[minum]
to drop (let fall)	**tercecer**	[tərtʃetʃer]
to dry (clothes, hair)	**mengeringkan**	[məneriŋkan]
to eat (vi, vt)	**makan**	[makan]
to end (~ a relationship)	**menghentikan**	[mənhentikan]
to excuse (forgive)	**memaafkan**	[memaʔafkan]
to exist (vi)	**ada**	[ada]
to expect (foresee)	**menduga**	[mənduga]
to explain (vt)	**menjelaskan**	[məndʒʲelaskan]
to fall (vi)	**jatuh**	[dʒʲatuh]
to fight (street fight, etc.)	**berkelahi**	[bərkelahi]
to find (vt)	**menemukan**	[mənemukan]
to finish (vt)	**mengakhiri**	[mənahiri]
to fly (vi)	**terbang**	[tərbaŋ]
to forbid (vt)	**melarang**	[melaraŋ]
to forget (vi, vt)	**melupakan**	[melupakan]
to forgive (vt)	**memaafkan**	[memaʔafkan]
to get tired	**lelah**	[lelah]
to give (vt)	**memberi**	[memberi]
to go (on foot)	**berjalan**	[bərdʒʲalan]
to hate (vt)	**membenci**	[membentʃi]
to have (vt)	**mempunyai**	[mempunjaj]
to have breakfast	**sarapan**	[sarapan]
to have dinner	**makan malam**	[makan malam]
to have lunch	**makan siang**	[makan siaŋ]
to hear (vt)	**mendengar**	[məndeŋar]
to help (vt)	**membantu**	[membantu]
to hide (vt)	**menyembunyikan**	[mənjembunjikan]
to hope (vi, vt)	**berharap**	[bərharap]
to hunt (vi, vt)	**berburu**	[bərburu]
to hurry (vi)	**tergesa-gesa**	[tərgesa-gesa]
to insist (vi, vt)	**mendesak**	[məndesaʔ]
to insult (vt)	**menghina**	[mənhina]
to invite (vt)	**mengundang**	[mənundaŋ]
to joke (vi)	**bergurau**	[bərgurau]
to keep (vt)	**menyimpan**	[mənjimpan]
to kill (vt)	**membunuh**	[membunuh]
to know (sb)	**kenal**	[kenal]

to know (sth)	tahu	[tahu]
to like (I like …)	suka	[suka]
to look at …	melihat …	[melihat …]

to lose (umbrella, etc.)	kehilangan	[kehilaŋan]
to love (sb)	mencintai	[mənʧintaj]
to make a mistake	salah	[salah]
to meet (vi, vt)	bertemu	[bərtemu]
to miss (school, etc.)	absen	[absen]

30. Verbs. Part 3

to obey (vi, vt)	mematuhi	[mematuhi]
to open (vt)	membuka	[membuka]
to participate (vi)	turut serta	[turut serta]
to pay (vi, vt)	membayar	[membajar]
to permit (vt)	mengizinkan	[məŋizinkan]

to play (children)	bermain	[bərmajn]
to pray (vi, vt)	bersembahyang, berdoa	[bərsembahjaŋ], [bərdoa]
to promise (vt)	berjanji	[bərʤˈanʤi]
to propose (vt)	mengusulkan	[məŋusulkan]
to prove (vt)	membuktikan	[membuktikan]
to read (vi, vt)	membaca	[membatʃa]

to receive (vt)	menerima	[mənerima]
to rent (sth from sb)	menyewa	[mənjewa]
to repeat (say again)	mengulangi	[məŋulaŋi]
to reserve, to book	memesan	[memesan]
to run (vi)	lari	[lari]

to save (rescue)	menyelamatkan	[mənjelamatkan]
to say (~ thank you)	berkata	[bərkata]
to see (vt)	melihat	[melihat]
to sell (vt)	menjual	[mənʤˈual]
to send (vt)	mengirim	[məŋirim]
to shoot (vi)	menembak	[mənembaʔ]

to shout (vi)	berteriak	[bərteriaʔ]
to show (vt)	menunjukkan	[mənunʤˈuʔkan]
to sign (document)	menandatangani	[mənandataŋani]
to sing (vi)	menyanyi	[mənjanji]
to sit down (vi)	duduk	[duduʔ]

to smile (vi)	tersenyum	[tərsenyum]
to speak (vi, vt)	berbicara	[bərbitʃara]
to steal (money, etc.)	mencuri	[mənʧuri]
to stop (please ~ calling me)	menghentikan	[məŋhentikan]
to study (vt)	mempelajari	[mempeladʒˈari]

to swim (vi)	berenang	[bərenaŋ]
to take (vt)	mengambil	[məŋambil]
to talk to …	bebicara dengan …	[bebitʃara deŋan …]
to tell (story, joke)	menceritakan	[məntʃeritakan]
to thank (vt)	mengucapkan terima kasih	[mənutʃapkan tərima kasih]
to think (vi, vt)	berpikir	[bərpikir]
to translate (vt)	menerjemahkan	[mənerdʒiemahkan]
to trust (vt)	mempercayai	[mempertʃajaj]
to try (attempt)	mencoba	[məntʃoba]
to turn (e.g., ~ left)	membelok	[membeloʔ]
to turn off	mematikan	[mematikan]
to turn on	menyalakan	[mənjalakan]
to understand (vt)	mengerti	[məŋerti]
to wait (vt)	menunggu	[mənuŋgu]
to want (wish, desire)	mau, ingin	[mau], [iŋin]
to work (vi)	bekerja	[bekerdʒia]
to write (vt)	menulis	[mənulis]

www.ingramcontent.com/pod-product-compliance
Lightning Source LLC
Chambersburg PA
CBHW070115070426
42448CB00039B/2871